GREAT SMOKIES

MYTHS & LEGENDS

THE TRUE STORIES BEHIND HISTORY'S MYSTERIES

MICHAEL R. BRADLEY

Globe
Pequot

Guilford, Connecticut

Globe
Pequot

An imprint of The Rowman & Littlefield Publishing Group, Inc.
4501 Forbes Blvd., Ste. 200
Lanham, MD 20706
www.rowman.com

Distributed by NATIONAL BOOK NETWORK

British Library Cataloguing in Publication Information available

Library of Congress Cataloging-in-Publication Data

Names: Bradley, Michael R. (Michael Raymond), 1940- author.
Title: Great Smokies myths and legends : the true stories behind history's mysteries / Michael R. Bradley.
Description: Guilford, Connecticut : Globe Pequot, [2020] | Includes bibliographical references and index. | Summary: "A look at some of Great Smoky Mountains National Park's most fascinating and compelling stories, from Sam Houston's childhood among the Cherokee to the mysterious 'road to nowhere.' "— Provided by publisher.
Identifiers: LCCN 2020033548 (print) | LCCN 2020033549 (ebook) | ISBN 9781493040261 (cloth : alk. paper) | ISBN 9781493040278 (electronic)
Subjects: LCSH: Great Smoky Mountains (N.C. and Tenn.)—History—Anecdotes. | Legends—Great Smoky Mountains (N.C. and Tenn.) | Great Smoky Mountains (N.C. and Tenn.)—Biography—Anecdotes. | Great Smoky Mountains National Park (N.C. and Tenn.)—History—Anecdotes.
Classification: LCC F443.G7 B73155 2020 (print) | LCC F443.G7 (ebook) | DDC 976.8/89—dc23
LC record available at https://lccn.loc.gov/2020033548
LC ebook record available at https://lccn.loc.gov/2020033549

∞™ The paper used in this publication meets the minimum requirements of American National Standard for Information Sciences—Permanence of Paper for Printed Library Materials, ANSI/NISO Z39.48-1992

Contents

Introduction..v

Chapter 1: Legendary Sam Houston.......................................1
Chapter 2: Abraham Enloe, Sixteenth President of the
United States?..14
Chapter 3: Mysterious, Murderous White Caps.................27
Chapter 4: Wicked Witch, Weary Woman, Misunderstood
Mother?...39
Chapter 5: Mythical Moonshine..51
Chapter 6: The Legend of Paul Bunyan, Smokies Style........65
Chapter 7: Ghost Towns Beneath Your Feet.......................78
Chapter 8: Horace Kephart...91
Chapter 9: The Legendary "Roamin' Man" of the Smokies:
Wiley Oakley...105
Chapter 10: The Mysterious Aura of Cades Cove................118
Chapter 11: Inspiring Images—Impenetrable Mystery........131
Chapter 12: The Disappearing Boomtown.........................144
Chapter 13: The Mysterious Road to Nowhere...................156
Chapter 14: The Story That Would Not Die.......................169

Bibliography..183
Index..189
About the Author...197

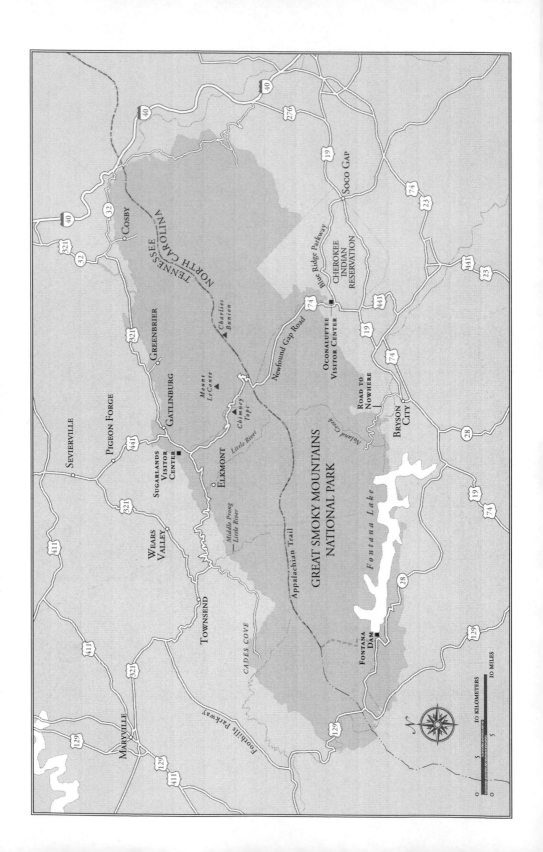

INTRODUCTION

My first visit to the Great Smoky Mountains was in 1956. As a college student I began making visits to the Smoky Mountains with the person who became my wife, and we have been returning to the mountains every year since. We have hiked many of the trails, spent many nights under the stars and clouds, and have met many wonderful and interesting people during our stays.

If, after sixty-two years, the Smoky Mountains still hold an allure for us, we must find them a very special place, and so they are. While locations have become familiar through repeated visits, no two stays in the Smokies are the same. The mountains are constantly revealing something new to us, something we have not seen before, some story or legend or piece of history we did not know.

The Great Smoky Mountains National Park is the most visited national park in the United States, with some ten million people entering the park each year. The park is located in the heart of the area called Appalachia and has preserved not only a sample of pristine scenery but also reminders of the people who lived in the mountains at an earlier time. Appalachia still has its own distinctive culture today, but while the "old ways" are remembered and respected, their practice has been overlaid by the ways of the current century. Going to the Smoky Mountains is stepping back in time, at least for a short while, and catching a glimpse of ways of life that have ceased to exist.

The plural "ways of life" is used deliberately because not all the people who have called the Smoky Mountains home have lived, thought, and believed the same.

Geologically, the Smoky Mountains are among the oldest mountains in North America,; thus, people have lived here for a very long time. No one is sure when the first people came to the area of the Great Smoky Mountains. Archaeologists and anthropologists date human habitation in the area to about 10,000 BC. Today, we do not have a name for these first people; because they left no written records, we do not know what they called themselves. At any rate, these settlers came to the Great Smoky Mountains long before the system of tribes developed that gives us our present-day names for Native American groups.

In some ways, the name "Native American" is not accurate because these people migrated to the Great Smoky Mountains from somewhere else. The Cherokee are the most recent of the Native American migrants. The Cherokee language belongs to the Iroquoian group of languages, a language found most frequently in Native American tribes in modern New England. No other tribe in the vicinity of the Great Smoky Mountains speaks any version of the Iroquoian language. It seems the Cherokee, at some time in the past, migrated south from the northeast Atlantic coast of North America and took possession of the area that became their homeland.

An Irishman called Galahan of Cowee established himself in the Cherokee homeland and became a trusted dealer who maintained good relations with the Cherokee. In 1775, when William Bartram came into the area making a biological survey of the native plants, Galahan told Bartram that the Cherokee territory covered about 40,000 square miles and that the tribe numbered about 20,000 people.

The Cherokee were a settled, as opposed to nomadic, people. They lived in towns and practiced agriculture to obtain a great part of their food. Favorite crops were corn (maize, as European explorers and settlers called it at first), squash, pumpkins, and beans. Since the Cherokee had no tools or weapons made of metal, they did not clear the ground but girdled trees to kill them and planted their crops among the standing dead trees. Girdling consisted of cutting through the bark and sap layers of the tree so that no sap reached the limbs from the roots, thus killing the tree. This process could be carried out with stone tools. All the crops favored by the Cherokee could be preserved by sun drying. Hunting was not a sport but was a way of providing animal protein and fats for their diet. The lack of firearms meant that most of the animals killed for food were small game, but large animals, such as deer, elk, and wood bison, were targets also. Fishing was done successfully by building fish traps in streams and then dipping fish out of the trap.

Since agriculture was the basis of the Cherokee economy, it should be no surprise that their towns were located in the valleys of rivers and large creeks where the soil was richer and crops grew more prolifically. The high mountain peaks did not have a large population of game animals; hunting, therefore, was focused on the streams flowing out of the mountains and the grassy coves on the sides of the heights. The Cherokee explored the high peaks and established trails through the mountains, but they lived near, rather than on, the mountains.

When European settlers began to arrive in the Cherokee territory, the Cherokee were vulnerable in two ways. The settlers brought with them an advanced technology—firearms, iron pots, steel tools—that functioned more efficiently than the traditional technology of the Cherokee. Just as is the case today, the more efficient technology appealed to the Cherokee, and they began to abandon many of their traditional ways in favor of the new "white" way of life. Second, the Cherokee were not very numerous. Galahan of Cowee told Bartram that the Cherokee territory extended over some 40,000 square miles although their population was only 20,000; that is, two square miles of land for every person. From the European point of view, much of this land was being wasted. If it were cleared and farmed in the European fashion, 40,000 square miles could support a huge population. From the Cherokee point of view, the land was being used. Some was used for farming, some for hunting, some for gathering, and the remainder was there for future use when their present fields lost their fertility.

In a clash between Stone Age technology and eighteenth-century technology, the odds favor the better technology; in a contest between a people numbering a few thousand and those numbering several hundred thousands, the odds favor the larger group.

The European settlers who came to the Great Smoky Mountains were those who could not find a place to settle along the seaboard. They came later in the period of exploration and settlement when the best land was already claimed, so they went west looking for opportunity. They came from Scotland, Ireland, and Germany for the most part, and they brought with them their own folkways and traditions. Some of them married Cherokee people because the Cherokee were hospitable and gracious in their relations with the newcomers. As the best lands in the Great Smoky Mountains were settled, the descendants of the first settlers moved farther up the slopes of the mountains, taking up farming on land that was more rocky and less productive. Over time, economics began to separate the "mountain people" from their more prosperous neighbors in the river valleys.

The restricted economy of the mountains also caused an outflow of young people who had to leave the old folks, the old home, and the old ways behind to earn a living. The Appalachian culture thus spread west and north, finding homes in Cleveland, Pittsburgh, Chicago, and many other midwestern urban centers.

Perhaps these fading family memories and tenuous cultural ties are some of the reasons so many people make their way to the Great Smoky Mountains each year. Perhaps this is why the myths and legends of the mountains appeal so strongly to modern readers.

Certainly, the spectacular scenery of the Great Smoky Mountains is reason enough to visit the area, but there is a haunting appeal about the music, the food, and the stories of the mountains. These things have kept me and my family coming back to the Great Smoky Mountains for more than sixty years. Listen to the myths, legends, and history contained in this book, and perhaps you will hear the mountains calling also.

CHAPTER 1

Legendary Sam Houston

An American Icon Rooted in the
Great Smoky Mountains

Sam Houston was president of an independent nation (the Republic of Texas), governor of two states (Tennessee and Texas), elected to the US Congress from two states (Tennessee and Texas), citizen of four nations (the United States, the Cherokee Nation, the Republic of Texas, the Confederate States), married three times, head of a Cherokee family, leader in war (War of 1812 and War of Texas Independence), opponent of secession, businessman, and land developer. The eighth-largest city in the United States is named for him, and his name is firmly associated with the state of Texas and its history; yet this American icon has roots in the Great Smoky Mountains and inextricable ties with the Cherokee people. Houston's life is a story of legendary turmoil, stress, and challenge, yet he always found the courage of spirit and the serenity of heart to face whatever came his way. Much of that strength can be traced to his identification with the Smoky Mountains and their Cherokee inhabitants.

Challenges came early in Houston's life; his father died when he was thirteen years old, and the next year his mother moved Sam, his five brothers, and three sisters to a farm near Maryville, Tennessee, just west of the present-day Great Smoky Mountains National Park. The family began to clear land and also opened a store in the growing village of Maryville, but Sam was not content to be a farmhand or a clerk in the family store. He had only a smattering of formal education, but he loved to read—his favorite book was *The Iliad*. Perhaps it was the dream of making his own heroic voyage that fueled his rebellion, or perhaps it was just a teenager's revolt against authority.

The family farm was only five miles from the boundary marking the beginning of lands belonging to the Cherokee, and Sam began to spend more and more time with his Native American neighbors. When his older brother insisted that Sam stay home and do his share to support the family, Sam ran away from home and went to live with the Cherokee. He is reported to have said he preferred measuring the size of a deer in the woods to measuring calico at the counter of a store. Of course, this act earned the lad quite a reputation among the other settlers and they said, only half-jokingly, that the strange business of running away to live with the Cherokee meant Sam might make a great chief, or, more likely, he would die in the madhouse. No one felt anything good was likely to come from the business.

WIKIMEDIA

Sam Houston: the raven, friend of the Cherokee, mountain man, and Texas hero

At age sixteen, Sam found himself living near a village led by Oolooteka, a tolerant and generous leader, who invited Houston to move into the village and to make his living as a member of the group. A life of fishing, hunting, trapping, and trading appealed to the young man, as did the welcoming, open, hospitable character of the Cherokee people. Oolooteka became a surrogate father for Houston and one of the individuals responsible for the character Houston developed. Many of the traits people admired in Houston—his bravery, oratorical skills, and leadership ability—were learned and honed during his stay with Oolooteka. The relationship between Houston and Oolooteka became so close that Houston was given a Cherokee name, Coloneh, "the raven." In Cherokee tradition the raven was a friend to all people who brought them the gift of fire, blackening itself in the effort. It's probably no coincidence that Houston himself had jet-black hair.

One of the people Houston met at his new home was a young woman named Tiana Rogers, the daughter of a white trader named John but usually called "Hell-Fire Jack," and Jennie Due, the sister of Oolooteka. John Rogers was a wealthy, well-educated man who had gained a reputation among the Cherokee for fair dealings. Tiana was described as "graceful as the bounding deer," and contemporaries agreed that she was "tall, slender, and beautiful." There is no historical record about what took place between Houston and Tiana, but given their ages, imagination can probably fill the gaps with reasonable accuracy. What is a matter of record is that they were married in 1830.

Economic realities forced Houston to leave the life he loved—he was in debt to some of the traders in the area to the tune of $300, and he could not earn enough to pay what he owed; therefore, in 1811 he returned to his family at Maryville and opened a school nearby to make some money. That occupation lasted just over a year. In 1812 the United States went to war with Great Britain in what some historians call "the second war of independence." The causes leading to war ranged from treatment of American sailors by the British navy to perceived attempts of the British government to foment unrest among the Native Americans on the frontier in an attempt to prevent further westward movement by American settlers.

The general appointed to protect what was then the southwestern portion of the United States was the popular leader Andrew Jackson. In response to Jackson's call for volunteers to move against the Creek Indians in what is today Alabama, Sam Houston left his schoolroom and became a soldier. So did many of the Cherokee. One of the overlooked factors in the destruction of the Native American hold on their land is the lack of unity among the Indians. Ancient tribal rivalries and animosities were exploited by the European settlers to weaken the various native groups. The War of 1812 provided another opportunity for this to happen. When Houston marched off to war, he found himself in the company of about six hundred Cherokee who had enlisted to fight their old enemy, the Creeks.

The decisive battle against the Creeks took place at Horseshoe Bend, a place the Creeks called Tohopeka, on the Tallapoosa River on March 27, 1814. The Creek defenders had built a breastwork across the open end of a bend in the river and were ready to put up a fierce defense of their position. While the white soldiers advanced against the breastwork, a group of Cherokees swam the river, took canoes the Creeks had pulled ashore on their side of the stream, and returned to ferry more Cherokee across the river to attack the Creeks from the rear. Hit from the front and rear, the Creeks suffered a crushing defeat. Houston was in the thick of the battle and paid a heavy price for his impetuous bravery: he suffered three wounds and very nearly died. Houston was shot in the arm and in one shoulder by rifles and was hit in the groin by an arrow. Sam Houston later wrote about his wounds and his return home:

> One (rifle) ball was extracted, but no attempt was made to extract the other, for the surgeon said it was unnecessary to torture me, since I could not survive until the next morning. I spent the night as soldiers do, who war in the wilderness, and carry provisions in their knapsacks for a week's march. Comforts were out of the question for any; but I received less attention than the others, for everybody looked on me as a dying man, and what could be done for any, they felt should be done for those who were likely to live. It was the darkest night of my life. On the following day I was started on a litter, with the other wounded, for Fort Williams, some sixty or seventy miles distant. Here I remained, suspended between life and death for a long time, neglected and exposed. I was finally brought back, through the Cherokee Nation, to my mother's home in Maryville, where I arrived in the latter part of May, nearly two months after the battle of the HorseShoe. . . . When I reached the home of my mother I was so worn to a skeleton that she declared she never would have known me except for my eyes, which still retained something of their wonted expression.

It is significant that Houston returned home through the Cherokee Nation. The supply line for Andrew Jackson's army ran from Fayetteville, Tennessee, through Alabama, and the Cherokee

Nation was farther to the east, so it seems that Houston was assisted by friends among the Cherokee even though they were unable to offer the medical care he needed. Back home, in the shadows of the Great Smoky Mountains, his slow path to recovery began.

One positive result of these serious wounds was that Andrew Jackson noticed the actions of Sam Houston, gave him a promotion, and named him a sub-agent to work with the Cherokees on behalf of the US government. Houston returned to the village of Oolooteka and Tiana and immediately began to use his influence to try to gain security for the Cherokee, leading a delegation to Washington, DC, to lobby Congress. Houston identified so completely with the Cherokee that even during his time in Washington he wore only the traditional clothing of the Cherokee, including a turban, their traditional head covering.

Part of the effort of this group was to try to get a guarantee that an area west of the Mississippi River would be set aside to become a permanently independent tribal nation. To some Native American leaders, it was obvious that there was no future for them east of the Mississippi; their lands and their people had become too fragmented and seemed doomed to disappear by assimilation with the white settlers. An independent tribal nation would allow them to preserve their culture and identity. Some of the Cherokee, including Oolooteka's brother, had moved west as early as 1782. In 1818, after agreeable arrangements were made by Houston, Oolooteka led his group of Cherokee to the West. On the death of his brother, Oolooteka became Principal Chief of the Cherokee-West.

Today, the forced removal of some of the Cherokee from their homes in the event known as the Trail of Tears is considered one of the great tragedies of US history, but in the early nineteenth century many of the Cherokee and their friends, such as Oolooteka and Sam Houston, thought moving west voluntarily was the wisest course for the Native Americans.

When Oolooteka's group moved to what is now Oklahoma, Houston desired to make a larger name for himself, so he studied law and entered politics. As a wounded hero of Horseshoe Bend and a friend of Andrew Jackson, Houston found it was an easy task to be elected to the US House of Representatives in 1824 and served two terms. As a congressman, Houston acted as a strong ally of Andrew Jackson, who was ready to run for the presidency of the United States. His support of Jackson led Houston to attack the integrity of John P. Erwin, a resident of Nashville who was the son-in-law of Jackson's political opponent Henry Clay. William A. White, a friend of Erwin, challenged Houston to a duel because of the insult. Houston went to The Hermitage, Jackson's home near Nashville, and spent several days in target practice. When the duel took place on September 22, 1826, White missed, Houston didn't, inflicting a serious wound on White. Because the actual duel had taken place in Kentucky, the home state of Henry Clay, an indictment was issued against Houston, but the governor of Tennessee refused to arrest the popular congressman, saying he had acted in self-defense.

In 1827 Houston ran for, and won, the office of governor of Tennessee. Then personal disaster struck. Sam Houston met and fell in love with Eliza Allen of Gallatin, Tennessee, the daughter of a wealthy and influential family. Sam was thirty-four, Eliza was nineteen. Their wedding was quite a social occasion, but less than two months later Eliza returned home and refused to rejoin Houston. The failure of the marriage touched off all manner of rumors and speculation, some of which continues to this day. Houston chose not to face the personal and political firestorm caused by the failure of the relationship; he resigned as governor and went west to live with the Cherokees. Since Houston was a close associate of Andrew Jackson, there was a strong possibility that the former Tennessee governor would continue to rise in the Democratic Party and become president of the United States. Now Houston's political career in Tennessee was at an end. Although he lived far from the Smoky Mountains, the people Houston had come to know during his years there now became his place of personal and psychological refuge.

According to one story, Houston told Oolooteka that the wound he had received in the groin at Horseshoe Bend had never healed and that it caused him such pain that he had been unable to consummate his marriage. Oolooteka then called for a Cherokee herbal doctor, who treated Houston's wound with poultices until the infection had subsided enough to permit probing the wound and the removal of an arrowhead. Whether or not this account is accurate, Houston did have children by both Tiana and by his last wife, whom he married in 1840.

Houston again expressed his identification with the Cherokee by dressing in traditional clothing and by living in seclusion from all white society. Rumors followed him, however, and it was reported in the East that he was drinking heavily; so much that news accounts began referring to him as "Big Drunk." However, the Indian translation of that name is in the Osage language, so the accuracy of the description is questionable since the Osage and the Cherokee were longtime enemies.

What is not in dispute is that he married Tiana. There had been no divorce from Eliza Allen, but Houston knew that relationship had come to an end in reality if not in the eyes of the law. The Cherokee had been wise enough to pass a law that white men marrying Cherokee women did not make the men eligible to inherit native-owned land. To show that he truly identified with the Cherokee, Houston requested and was granted the status of a naturalized citizen in the Cherokee Nation. Only then did he wed Tiana, probably in the village where Oolooteka lived. The couple established a home in a large log cabin that they named "The Wigwam Neosho," and they worked to earn a living by opening a trading post, farming, raising livestock, and growing apples.

Life among the Cherokee suited Houston. He enjoyed the open hospitality of his neighbors and friends, and he began to participate in the political life of the people. In public speech, Houston usually called the Cherokee "the red people" or simply "Indians." Oolooteka, however, used the term Native Americans on many, though not all, occasions. Houston championed the cause of his fellow Cherokee citizens in a series of articles he wrote for the *Arkansas Gazette* in June and December 1830. In these articles he blasted the actions of US government agents who did not honestly administer the funds promised by the government to the Cherokee in return for their moving west. Houston also undertook another trip to Washington to argue the Cherokee cause. On this trip Houston continued his practice of wearing the traditional Cherokee clothing. This attire was considered highly inappropriate by

Secretary of War John C. Calhoun, who scolded Houston about his dress. Houston let it be known that "I am no longer a white man. I have left those who were my people and have joined those who are now my people."

Also during this trip, on April 13, 1832, Houston picked a fight with Representative William Stanbery of Ohio. Stanbery had earlier made some remarks in a speech that Houston felt were insulting. When the two men encountered one another on a Washington street, Houston attacked Stanbery with his hickory walking stick and the congressman drew a pistol. The pistol misfired, and Houston administered a severe beating to Stanberry. Houston was arrested and brought to trial before the House of Representatives, where his defense attorney was Francis Scott Key. A month later Houston was given a reprimand and a small fine, but he succeeded in placing the plight of the Cherokee before the public.

Back home, Houston became restless; the political situation in Texas was unsettled. A stream of Anglo settlers had been entering the Mexican territory for two decades and there was a growing movement to break away from the government in Mexico City and form an independent nation. Houston saw an opportunity in this situation both for himself and for the Cherokee people. He told Tiana that he wanted to move south and she said for him to go; she would stay where she was and wait to see what happened in Texas. The two never lived together again. In 1840, two years after Tiana died, Houston married for the third time, becoming the husband of Margaret Moffette Lea. She was twenty-one, he was forty-seven. They had eight children, the last being born in 1860 when Sam was sixty-seven. When Houston headed for Texas in 1832, the Great

Smoky Mountains were receding farther and farther behind him, but the Cherokee people were still very much present in his heart. As early as 1785 some Cherokee had asked permission from the Spanish governor of Mexico to settle in territory he governed. The governor passed on the request to the King of Spain, who granted a royal charter to a group led by an influential leader named Konnetue. This group of Cherokee settlers was soon followed by others until there were six Cherokee towns in what is now Arkansas and Missouri. The Louisiana Purchase of 1803 placed these towns back inside the territory of the United States, so a Cherokee leader called Bowl petitioned the government of now-independent Mexico for a place to live. Bowl led his followers to settle near what became Dallas, Texas. By the time Houston moved to Texas in 1832, there were several hundred members of the Cherokee Nation living there. According to one study of Houston, it is likely that he intended to establish an empire of Native Americans in Texas and play a role in its government. For such a venture, the support of the Cherokee would be vital. If this was his plan it did not succeed as intended, although several hundred Cherokee did join the Texas army during the War of Texas Independence.

The movement for Texas independence soon was dominated by Anglo settlers, but Houston played a major role as leader of the tiny army fighting for independence from Mexico. The death of all the defenders of the Alamo gave the psychological impetus for the victory the Texas forces won at San Jacinto, now part of the city of Houston, on April 21, 1836. Houston was wounded and had his horse killed under him, but won a total victory in a battle that lasted an astonishing eighteen minutes. Riding into battle,

Houston had draped around his shoulders a blanket woven in a traditional Cherokee pattern.

As the hero of the struggle for independence, Sam Houston was elected President of the Republic of Texas. Any dream of establishing a homeland for Native Americans, especially the Cherokee, was now gone, but Houston used his position as president to work for good relations between whites and Native Americans. President Houston held frequent conferences with leaders of the many Native groups in territory claimed by Texas. These meetings were characterized by attempts to rectify past wrongs and to establish trust. Houston gave orders to stop white settlers from trespassing on land set aside for the various tribes, but he also sent out military forces to stop raids by Indians on settlements. Among the fiercest of the raiders were the Comanches. Turning to old friends, Houston named the Cherokee leader Bowl as the official representative to negotiate on behalf of the Texas government.

Houston's attitude toward Native Americans was in marked contrast with that of most of the people of his day, many of whom favored extermination or, at least, banishing all of them to some remote area. In response to such views, Houston publicly stated, "I will punish any man who does injustice to the Indians. I have known them from my boyhood. They are a brave, honest, upright people." The lessons of tolerance learned in the Great Smoky Mountains followed Sam Houston for the rest of his life.

CHAPTER 2

Abraham Enloe, Sixteenth President of the United States?

An Enduring Smoky Mountain Legend

Today Abraham Lincoln is one of the best known of all US presidents, one with a massive heritage and enduring popularity among the public. But this was not the case during his lifetime. While serving as president, Lincoln was often called an ape, a baboon, a scheming tyrant, and many things not fit for print in a respectable book. Among the many rumors circulated about President Lincoln was the assertion that he was not a Lincoln at all, nor was he from Kentucky, but instead his father was a man named Abraham Enloe who lived in North Carolina. This legend about the sixteenth president persists today and has ties to the Great Smoky Mountains.

According to the old story, Abraham Enloe was a prosperous farmer who lived in Rutherford County, North Carolina. Around

The site of the Enloe Farm is today the Oconoluftee Visitor Center.

1800 Enloe brought a twelve-year-old orphan, Nancy Hanks, to his farm as an indentured servant. Being an indentured servant was very common in the United States from the seventeenth century colonial times until the early nineteenth century, when the practice began to die out. As an indentured servant, one sold their labor for a period of time, seven years being the usual term, to another person in exchange for room, board, and clothing. Many people learned a trade by being an indentured servant to a blacksmith or weaver, for example. Keep in mind that these servants sold their labor, not their persons; indentured servants were protected by the terms of their contracts and, thus, were free people, not slaves.

In about 1806 the Enloe family, including their servant Nancy Hanks, moved to the Oconoluftee section of the Smoky

Mountains. In fact, their farm was located at the present site of the Oconoluftee Visitor Center for the Great Smoky Mountains National Park. The Enloe family had a daughter, also named Nancy, who fell in love with a young man named Thompson, of whom the family did not approve. Nancy Enloe disregarded the wishes of her family and ran off with the young man. They married and moved to the western part of Kentucky, which had just opened up good land for settlement.

After two years, Nancy Enloe Thompson came back home for a visit. There she found the household in turmoil. Their servant, Nancy Hanks, had given birth to a baby not long after Nancy had eloped, and the child, now two years old, had a very strong resemblance to Abraham Enloe. Obviously, Mrs. Enloe was not happy about this situation and she insisted that Nancy Hanks and her son had to leave Oconoluftee as soon as possible. The departure of Nancy Enloe Thompson for her home in Kentucky offered the chance the family had been waiting for. Nancy Hanks and her son went back to Kentucky with Nancy Enloe. Back at her home, Nancy Enloe Thompson arranged for a man named Thomas Lincoln to marry Nancy Hanks and take on the responsibility for her son as well. Thus, Abraham Enloe, Jr., became Abraham Lincoln. Or so goes the story, and there are several variations of it.

The story that Abraham Enloe was the real father of Abraham Lincoln appeared in 1860 when Lincoln was nominated for president. Until that time Lincoln had been a rather obscure figure in Illinois political circles and was not known to a national audience. The origin of the 1860 story was a visit paid by a Mr. Davis of Illinois, who had traveled to North Carolina, where he had been born.

Davis was staying in the home of a Dr. Edgerton, who was a relative of Mrs. Abraham Enloe.

Davis claimed to be a friend of Lincoln and told Dr. Edgerton that Lincoln admitted he "was of Southern extraction and that his name was, or ought to have been, Enloe, but he had always gone by the name of his stepfather."

This story, which a historian would label "hearsay evidence," was given impetus by Lincoln himself. Following his nomination for the presidency Lincoln was approached by J. S. Scripps, a reporter for the *Chicago Tribune*. Scripps asked Lincoln a question about his background, including his family. Lincoln replied, "It is a waste of time to inquire about my early life, it can be condensed into a single sentence found in *Grey's Elegy*, 'The short and simple annals of the poor.' That is my life and that's all you or anyone else can make of it." In another conversation about his family, Lincoln talked about his father, Thomas, and his grandfather, Abraham (not Enloe) but admitted he knew almost nothing about his grandfather and thus not much about his father. In this conversation, like that with Scripps, Lincoln never mentioned Nancy Hanks.

William H. Herndon, at one time the law partner of Abraham Lincoln, wrote a book about Lincoln some years after Lincoln's death. Writing from memory, Herndon recounted a conversation between the two that occurred while they were traveling to Menard County, Illinois, to try a case. The case involved a question about hereditary traits, and Lincoln commented that illegitimate children were often stronger and smarter than those born in wedlock. As an example, Lincoln cited his mother, who was the daughter of Lucy Hanks and an unknown farmer from Virginia. Lincoln felt he had inherited his physical characteristics from his mother, who was tall, while his father, Thomas, was average height. Lincoln also felt his mental agility came from his mother.

There is historical evidence that makes believable the idea that Nancy Hanks was herself born to a single mother. A grand jury in Mercer County, Kentucky, gave a "true bill" verdict against Lucy Hanks (meaning that the grand jury felt there was enough evidence to warrant a trial), and other records show several children born to Hanks females who were not married. In the nineteenth century having an unwed mother in one's family tree would have had serious social and political consequences, which is likely the reason Lincoln had so little to say about his mother. Aside from the rumors and stories, a written record from Washington County, Kentucky, shows that Thomas Lincoln received a marriage license to marry Nancy Hanks on June 11, 1806. Reverend Jesse Head signed the license and returned it to the courthouse, as required by law, on June 12, 1806, confirming that he had performed the wedding ceremony. Tax records show Thomas Lincoln to have been in Kentucky as early as 1786. These historical records are countered by stories of elderly people who, in the years following Lincoln's assassination, said they remembered Nancy Hanks before she married Thomas Lincoln and that she had a child at the time they were wed. For example, Austin Gallaher was a neighbor of Thomas and Nancy Lincoln and swore that, as a boy, he walked to school with Abraham Lincoln in 1812; he remembered the date because Lincoln and he were fording a flooded creek on the way to school and Lincoln lost his footing. Gallaher saved him from being swept away by the swollen current. Obviously, the Abraham Lincoln spoken of by Austin Gallaher was not born in 1809, Lincoln's "official birth date," but was several years older. The lack of historical records about Nancy Hanks Lincoln, and the absence of a birth record for Abraham Lincoln, creates an aura of doubt that allows stories and legends to flourish.

One remaining fact about Nancy Hanks Lincoln is that she died on December 5, 1818. On the frontier, where the Lincoln family lived, cows were allowed to wander free, and the milk cows were called up to be milked. Roaming free, the cows ate whatever came before them; one such plant was white snakeroot, a wild-flower found widely in the eastern United States, including the Great Smoky Mountains National Park. This plant contains a mild poison, but because cows chew their cud, chewing and partially digesting their food over and over, the poison becomes concentrated in milk. Nancy Lincoln drank contaminated milk and died as a result. Abraham Lincoln was nine years old at the time. His mother was buried on the family farm. A year later Thomas Lincoln went to Elizabethtown, Kentucky, and married Sarah Bush Johnston, a widow with three children of her own.

Abraham Lincoln seemed to like his stepmother a great deal and she, in turn, encouraged him to get as much education as possible in the developing frontier community where they lived. In 1830 the family left Indiana for Illinois, and Abraham Lincoln began to make a living on his own, eventually becoming a lawyer and a political leader. The curious note in this is that the grave of Nancy Hanks Lincoln was abandoned and became overgrown in weeds and brush. Even after he had become a successful and wealthy attorney, Abraham Lincoln did not see to it that the burial place of his mother was cared for, and he never placed a tombstone on her grave. It was not until 1925 when the state of Indiana took charge of the property and began to maintain it that a marker was erected over Nancy Hanks Lincoln's grave. Thomas Lincoln died in January 1851. Abraham Lincoln had written to him during his final illness, but the letter has a cold and impersonal tone. Abraham made no effort to attend his father's funeral, nor did he provide a stone marker for the grave. It is said that Abraham Lincoln visited his father's grave following his election to the presidency and carved the initials T. L. on a piece of wood to serve as a marker for the grave. A stone was placed on the grave by a group of local citizens following Abraham Lincoln's assassination.

This cavalier attitude toward both his mother and father continues to fuel speculation about Abraham Lincoln's relationship with his parents. Was Thomas really his father? Why was he so reticent about his mother? Did he think more highly of his stepmother than of his mother because Sarah Bush Johnston Lincoln recognized his potential and helped him achieve a much better life by helping him with his education? However, Lincoln did not attend her funeral nor place a marker on her grave, either. For those who are fascinated by alternative histories, such questions always lead back to Abraham Enloe.

As often is the case with presidents who are assassinated, Abraham Lincoln's public popularity grew enormously following his death. Overnight, even those who had bitterly opposed Lincoln's policies when he was alive found only good things to say about him. Robert Lincoln, the only surviving son of the president, became Secretary of the Treasury and let it be known he had political aspirations to follow in the footsteps of his father. Obviously, Robert Lincoln was anxious to see only good things said and written about his father. Many writers were anxious to write about such a popular figure as Abraham Lincoln, and those who had been close to him were even more anxious to tell their stories. One of these writers was William H. Herndon, once law partner to Abraham Lincoln, and another was Ward Lamon.

Abraham Lincoln met Ward Lamon during the 1850s when Lamon was the prosecuting attorney in an area of Illinois where Lincoln practiced law. When Lincoln was elected president, Lamon was appointed US Marshal for the District of Columbus and took on the role of bodyguard to the president (the Secret Service would not be created for several decades). On Lincoln's death, Lamon resigned his government post and returned to the practice of law while using his free time to write *The Life of Abraham Lincoln: From His Birth to His Inauguration as President*. The book came on the market in 1872 and contained many revelations about President Lincoln that ran counter to his post-assassination reputation. Among other statements, Lamon pointed out that "Mr. Lincoln was never a member of any church, nor did he believe in the divinity of Christ, or the inspiration of the Scriptures." According to those who question Lincoln's paternity, this unfavorable book by a close and devoted associate of the dead president led to a concerted effort to quash all talk about Nancy Hanks and Abraham Enloe. Robert Lincoln wanted to make a run for the presidency in 1876 and he was said to feel the need to polish the reputation of his father to enhance his chances. Suddenly, all writers who had questions about Abraham Enloe or about Nancy Hanks Lincoln were met with a very cold reception and were refused permission to do research in the Lincoln archives.

As with so much of the legend about Abraham Enloe, there are just enough facts in the allegations to give the shadow of credence to the idea that Abraham Lincoln was really Abraham Enloe. In the Smoky Mountains, while Abraham Lincoln was being elected president, while the Civil War raged, while the Reconstruction era tried to stitch the nation back together, the Enloe family was going about the affairs of daily living and the old stories about Nancy Hanks continued to be told. Abraham Enloe had sixteen children; the youngest son, Wesley Enloe, was alive during the post–Civil War period and was willing to talk to anyone interested about the family tradition concerning Nancy Hanks. Wesley was born after the alleged affair involving Nancy Hanks had taken place, but he repeated stories his older brothers and sisters had told him. The increasing availability of cameras led to another attempt to link the Enloe family with Abraham Lincoln; photographs of Wesley Enloe as a young man are said by some to bear a striking resemblance to Abraham Lincoln before Lincoln grew a beard. It was during this time that people began to make comments about the fact that Thomas Lincoln was only five feet, ten inches in height and never showed any indication of having more than average intelligence, if that. Abraham Enloe was well over six feet, weighed about 200 pounds, and was locally considered to be well educated. Nancy Hanks was a little above average in height for a female of her day, but was not thought to be unusually tall.

The rumors and traditional stories about an Enloe-Lincoln connection became so prevalent that in 1899, thirty-four years after Lincoln's assassination, James H. Cathey of Sylvia, North Carolina, began to collect firsthand accounts from those old enough to remember Abraham Enloe and who had been alive during Lincoln's presidency. Cathey produced a book based on these accounts, *Stranger Than Fiction: True Genesis of a Wonderful Man*, while a second edition was produced under the title *The Genesis of Lincoln*. In his books Cathey presents a great deal of circumstantial evidence and many hearsay accounts, all of which would be of questionable value to an academically trained historian, but which certainly fueled, and continue to spark, debates in online forums and history discussion sites.

In Cathey's books, Wesley Enloe says that he was born after the matter between Nancy Hanks and his father arose, but he had a strong memory of Nancy Hanks being mentioned often in family discussions, although his father never had anything to say on the matter. However, Wesley Enloe had no doubt that Nancy Hanks was sent to Kentucky because she became pregnant by his father. Another of Cathey's interviewees was Joseph Collins, who recounted a story told him years before by a "Judge Gilmore" who claimed to know Nancy Hanks before she left North Carolina. Judge Gilmore claimed that Nancy Hanks had a small child when she left for Kentucky, where she married a man named Lincoln.

Judge Gilmore also recounted that he had met a traveling salesman, Philip Wells, who told of staying overnight at the Enloe farm and being told that relations in the family were strained at the time because of the presence of a servant girl named Nancy Hanks. When Wells came back to the area some months later, the servant girl had been sent to another community to have a baby and was being sent to Kentucky to find a husband.

A final story in Cathey's account involved an attorney named Davidson who probated Abraham Enloe's estate. Davidson said that just after the close of the Civil War a man came to his office and introduced himself as the son of Nancy Enloe Thompson, a daughter of Abraham Enloe who was a member of the family at the same time that Nancy Hanks had lived with the Enloes. The man had been appointed a US Indian agent by President Lincoln, although he was a Democrat. When the attorney asked why Lincoln would appoint a Democrat to such a highly paid post, the reply was that Lincoln was under a great obligation to the Enloe family and this had been his way of meeting that obligation.

The books by James Cathey led to the publication of others. In 1920 William E. Barton published *The Paternity of Abraham Lincoln*, in which he defended the traditional account of Lincoln's parents being Thomas Lincoln and Nancy Hanks. This account was met by a challenge written by James Caswell, *Abraham Lincoln: A North Carolinian*.

The timing of the publication of these books is significant because the US Congress was debating whether or not a national memorial to Abraham Lincoln should be constructed in Washington, DC, where it should be placed, and how much it should cost. Work on the Lincoln Memorial began in 1914 and was completed in 1922. At the same time as the Lincoln Memorial was being erected, a final link in the Enloe-Lincoln legend was being built at Pigeon Forge. Around 1920, two unmarried brothers, Robert Bruce and Roger Lafayette Mullendore, commissioned Louis

The last of the Enloe family to live in the area occupied this house.

Buckner, a widely acclaimed African American designer and crafts-man, to design a house for them. This was the last known commis-sion accepted by Buckner, who died of a heart attack in 1924.

When the house was completed, the two brothers moved in accompanied by their mother, Laura Enloe Mullendore, and an unmarried sister, Dialtha Melinda Mullendore, called "Ninnie." The family lived in the house for about fifty years, by which time the two women had died and the brothers were ready to sell their farm and their old home. The real estate was quite valuable because by the 1970s the Great Smoky Mountains National Park had estab-lished itself as the most popular national park in the nation, and the demand for tourist facilities had spread to Pigeon Forge. The house was a gem of bungalow-style architecture and still contained original interior woodwork by Louis Buckner, including built-in cabinets, cupboards, and carved mantles. The new owners of the house undertook renovations, being careful to preserve the original features; while removing an interior wall that had been added later, the builders discovered a photograph of the Mullendores' great-grandfather, Abraham Enloe.

Was the sixteenth president of the United States really Abraham Enloe? The unanimous opinion of academically trained historians is that he was not. But there are enough gaps in the family tree of Abraham Lincoln to allow questions to continue to be raised, especially by those who love a good Smoky Mountain legend.

Note: The major flaw in the Abraham Enloe legend is that Abraham Lincoln had an older sister. There is no mention of her in the Enloe account; it is as if she did not exist. However, the Enloe account continues to have its supporters. Not far to the east of the Great Smoky Mountains National Park is the town of Bostic, North Carolina, which is home to the Lincoln Center, a not-for-profit association that maintains a museum of items related to the Enloe family and the history of the area. The center sponsors lectures on the topic of the Enloe-Lincoln connection, and has marked the remaining foundation stones of a house where Nancy Hanks is said to have given birth to Abraham Lincoln. Appropriately, the house remains are located on what has long been named "Lincoln Hill," which is on the banks of the well-named Puzzle Creek.

Local historian Jerry Goodnight has published two books on the subject: *The Tarheel Lincoln* in 2003 and *Searching for Lincoln* in 2008. The town of Bostic also sponsors a Lincoln Festival each spring.

CHAPTER 3

Mysterious, Murderous White Caps

W ell, I say such a woman as that ought not be allowed to live amongst respectable folks! She is a loose woman with no morals at all. Just by being here she is a temptation to our husbands and sons and if we don't do something then we are helping her in her evil ways."

"What I think is, if that no-'count husband of hers would go to the field and work their crop instead of laying off in the woods hunting or fishing—when he ain't making whiskey—they would be a lot better off and maybe would live better lives."

So it started. Concerned about the influence of those who did not measure up to community standards of behavior and morality, a few people in the scattered villages and rural communities of Sevier County, just north of today's Great Smoky Mountains National Park, turned to the old practice of vigilantism, enforcing what they knew to be community standards and what they thought should be law by using violence and threats of violence against those who violated those standards. The practice would come to be called "whitecapping," and those who practiced it were "White Caps" because they wore masks covering their heads and faces.

Today millions of visitors turn south off Interstate 40 and drive toward the Great Smoky Mountains National Park, passing through Sevierville and Pigeon Forge, unaware of the bloody conflict that cursed this area in the 1890s. But once this now lovely, very commercial corridor was home to the mysterious, murderous White Caps. Who were they? What did they do?

In the summer of 1892, Julia Ramsey, a young woman living in the Emerts Cove area of Sevier County, received a warning via a note accompanied by a bundle of switches that her personal behavior was not acceptable to the White Caps of her neighborhood. The writer warned Julia that if she did not change her ways she would receive a visit one night soon. Already six women had been dragged from their beds and whipped unmercifully with switches because they were thought to be promiscuous. Somehow, Julia's father found out the night the White Caps were planning their raid and he asked his neighbor, Eli Williamson, to stay with the family that night to protect Julia.

About midnight, hoofbeats were heard in the yard of the Ramsey dwelling, followed by loud footsteps tramping across the front porch and a pounding on the door. Men shouted loudly for Julia to come outside and face her punishment. Instead, the door opened and Ramsey and Williamson opened fire on the White Caps. One of the night riders, Llewellyn Sneed, cried out in pain and had to be helped to his horse as the attackers swiftly left the premises. Taken to a doctor the next day, Sneed was told he would be crippled in one leg permanently as a result of the wound.

Two weeks later, William Sneed, brother of the crippled Llewellyn, and Huse Romines approached the home of Eli Williamson, who lived alone. Romines entered the house by the front door while Sneed went to the back. Williamson attempted to reach his gun but was shot in the head by Sneed before he could defend himself.

Williamson's murder shocked the Emerts Cove community. While some people disapproved of some of Julia Ramsey's activities, most people felt she would have to answer to a higher power in the end and that they were not to be her judges. Certainly, murdering a man who had helped a neighbor defend his daughter against night riders was a violation of community values. John Springs, a prosperous farmer who began to speak openly and forcefully in opposition to the White Caps, received so much local support that there were no more night riding incidents in the Emerts Cove community. But this was not the end of the White Caps. An attempt to indict William Sneed for the murder of Williamson failed when the grand jury brought in a verdict of "no true bill"—that is, the grand jury did not believe there was enough evidence against Sneed to justify a trial by judge and jury. This grand jury finding convinced many people in Sevier County that the White Caps had friends in high places who could sway the courts. This assumption was correct.

Circuit Court Judge W. R. Hicks was always sympathetic to defendants accused of White Cap activities, and Sheriff E. M. Wynn was the father of two known members of the White Caps, one of whom was hanged for murder.

The White Caps thus represented two groups of people. There were men of wealth and influence who agreed with the group but who did not choose to take a hand in actual night riding. They did provide money to pay legal fees, post bond for those who were arrested, and provide clandestine help with selecting members of both grand and trial juries. These supporters gave some aura of respectability to the group and encouraged others to join. The second group represented in the White Cap movement comprised those who were ready and willing to go night riding and to inflict punishment on those they felt deserved it. The arrangement between those who might be called "supporters" and those who were active "raiders" was so effective that no person accused of White Cap activity ever failed to make bond and none of the members ever skipped bond. Unfortunately, the failure of the White Caps to establish a lasting base in Emerts Cove did not prevent them from being more successful in other communities.

Popular imagination today looks at the decade of the 1890s as an idyllic time when life was simpler, more wholesome, and quite stable. Actually, the 1890s were a time of turmoil and change that entailed a good deal of social unrest across the entire nation. The economic status of agriculture was declining as the national economy became more and more oriented toward industry; therefore, across the nation farmers felt they were being left out of growing prosperity. Industrialists favored having US currency based on government possession of gold, making interest rates on loans high, while farmers favored including silver as part of the basis for the national monetary system. Using both silver and gold to support the economy would lower interest rates and help farmers. Several farm organizations, such as the Grange (an agricultural fraternal organization), became politically active in an attempt to change the economic situation.

Their influence helped split the Democratic Party in 1896 and produced the Populist Movement, which demanded that government economic policy favor the working class.

With the growth of cities came increased immigration, which caused some "old Americans" to feel threatened by the economic and political influence being exercised by "new Americans." The growth of cities and industrial jobs also caused a migration of African Americans to northern cities, where they competed with recent immigrants for jobs. The rise in racial tensions led to thirty-five states, including those on the West Coast, to pass racial segregation laws, a practice upheld by the Supreme Court of the United States in 1896 in the case *Plessy v. Ferguson.*

Railroads were rapidly changing the face of the nation, making possible rapid travel and the nationwide distribution of imported goods. Of course, if one lived in an area not served by a railroad, life remained much as it had been sixty years earlier, with travel and commerce using dirt roads or riverboats. This led to the "up to date" railroad towns looking down their noses at the "country bumpkins" and "hicks" who lived in the rural and small-town areas. Sevier County, with no railroad, was part of the left-behind sector of society while nearby Knoxville, with both river and rail transportation, represented the progressive "bright lights of the city" sector.

The activities of the White Caps in adjacent Sevier County were embarrassing to the business community of Knoxville because the latter was attempting to attract northern timber companies to move into the Smoky Mountains, which in turn would bring more jobs and a subsequent bump in tax revenues to the local economy.

These nationwide social tensions led to outbreaks of night riding in numerous places, especially in rural communities. Concerned and upset with the speed of social change, people turned to vigilantism in an attempt to solve problems or to release their raw emotions.

Mrs. Mary Breeden lived with her son, Jess, and two daughters, Bell and Martha, in an isolated part of Sevier County. In May, 1893, a band of eight White Caps came to their house and while four held guns on Jess, the other four proceeded to whip Bell and Martha for their "unbecoming behavior." When Mrs. Breeden protested the treatment of her daughters the night riders turned on her and beat her until she was bloody and collapsed. The two daughters, younger and stronger, recovered, but Mary Breeden was bedridden. Her wounds became infected and the local residents had exhausted their ability to help her with herbal medicines and home remedies. In desperation Jess rode several miles to ask Dr. Henderson for help.

J. A. Henderson was a graduate of Bellevue Medical College in New York City, one of the best medical schools in the nation at that time. When he arrived at the Breeden home, he found Mary so weak and her wounds so infected he could do nothing for her except give her painkillers. As the doctor administered what treatment he could, he talked with the family about their horrific experience. The description of their encounter with the White Caps so disgusted him that he resolved to put down the organization. Somehow, Dr. Henderson found a spy who infiltrated the White Caps and began to give him information about their plans. Others who agreed with Henderson formed a group called the "Blue Bills" because they wore baseball caps with blue bills. When the spy informed the Blue Bills that the White Caps planned to raid a home and flog someone, they would turn out men to guard the home or to ambush the White Caps as they rode to their destination.

At times this conflict between the White Caps and the Blue Bills took on the aspects of a comic opera, with each group learning the plans of the other, changing their plans, and then both deciding to do nothing. At times the conflict was deadly. Near the community of Henderson Springs, a well-known summer resort of the 1890s, a group of White Caps was riding to the home of a prospective victim while four Blue Bills, in groups of two, were riding to the same destination. The White Caps passed the leading pair of Blue Bills, who did not recognize their opponents in the darkness. The second pair of Blue Bills stopped the men approaching them and shots were fired. One of the Blue Bills, M. V. Llewellyn, was wounded and another, Elijah Helton, was killed while two White Caps were killed and the rest ran.

An election for sheriff had taken place just prior to the altercation at Henderson Springs. The primary issue of concern was what to do about the White Caps. The incumbent sheriff was opposed by E. M. Wynn and by businessman and known White Cap opponent Thomas Filmore Maples. In the hotly contested race, the vote count declared Maples winner by 147 votes. Sheriff Maples appointed Thomas Davis as deputy sheriff to help him clean up the county.

For the time and place, Davis was well educated, having attended Carson College for one term and Knoxville Business College for a year. He had been a schoolteacher, farmer, and small businessman, and he was a lifelong Democrat. Appointing a

Democrat to office was unheard of in East Tennessee; the divided loyalties of the Civil War had not disappeared—Republicans were still identified with support for the Union, while Democrats were still associated with the Confederacy. Sheriff Maples's appointment of Davis indicated that the situation demanded action across party lines. Soon the two men had arrested thirteen members of the White Caps.

Arrests are deterrents only if they are followed by court convictions. In this case, none of the men arrested came to trial because the grand jury refused to return "true bills," saying there was enough evidence of a crime to proceed to a jury trial. The White Caps did become somewhat more cautious, beginning to use secret passwords and symbols by which members could recognize each other, but they also became bolder, with many of their members engaging in common crimes, especially robbery of elderly people who lived in isolated places. Such actions began to turn community sentiment against the White Caps.

Some members of the White Caps began to use the organization to achieve personal goals. J. W. Catlett had a tenant living on his farm whom Catlett wanted to remove from his rented property. Catlett also had as tenants William and Laura Whaley; one night he went to the Whaley cabin and forced Laura to write a threatening letter to the tenant who was reluctant to leave his land. Once the letter was written, Catlett coerced Laura to swear the White Cap oath, which promised she would forever hold her action a secret on pain of death. Laura, however, was troubled about her involvement in threatening another family and talked with some members of the community she trusted about her action. Word of her remorse and the likelihood of Laura becoming a witness against the White Caps led to tragedy.

On the night of December 28, 1896, Pleasant "Pleas" Wynn and Catlett Tipton went to the Whaley cabin. Bursting into the main room they found William and Laura in bed with their new-born daughter, Molly. In an adjacent room was Lizzie Chandler, Laura's sister, who was staying with the Whaleys to help care for the infant. William was ill and was shot before he could make any move to defend his family. Laura asked only to be allowed to hand Molly to her sister before she was killed. For some reason, Wynn and Tipton left Lizzie unharmed. The murder of the Whaley family disgusted large segments of the community.

Lizzie Chandler was taken into protective custody by Deputy Sheriff Davis. On market day when most people came to town, she stood in an upstairs window of a hotel overlooking the public square from where she pointed out Wynn and Tipton as the men who had murdered the Whaleys. Davis soon arrested Wynn and Tipton on a charge of murder, and J. W. Catlett and Bob Wade were arrested as accomplices, since there was evidence that Catlett had paid Wynn to commit the murders and that Wade had known about the plan. All four men were soon out on bail, and Sheriff Maples and Deputy Sheriff Davis realized they needed help. Davis traveled to Nashville, the state capital, and lobbied the legislature successfully for two pieces of legislation. The first outlawed groups formed for the purpose of clandestine violations of the law, and the second moved Sevier County to a different judicial district. Supported with these two bills, Davis returned to Sevier County and brought Wynn and Tipton before a new judge, Thomas A. R.

Nelson, Jr., who revoked bail and sent them to jail until the next session of court. Nelson was an experienced judge and, as the son of a prominent Unionist, widely respected in the community. When the court convened, Wynn and Tipton were indicted for murder and were ordered to be held for trial in November 1897. John Springs, who had opposed the White Caps since their earliest days, was foreman of the jury that indicted the two.

The town of Sevierville was full of people when the trial began. In an attempt to secure an impartial jury, 1,200 men had been called to be examined for possible jury service.

Among those called was a farmer and Primitive Baptist minister, Israel Alexander Hatcher. The Hatcher family was well respected in their community, Hatcher's Mountain, which was located in Wears Valley just a few miles north of present-day Townsend, Tennessee. Israel was born in 1860 and grew up during the tumultuous Civil War years; during and following the war, his family had provided for several Union soldiers. While still a young man he felt the call to become a minister and served several small churches in the area near his family home, riding horseback several miles to reach some of them. Because of his reputation for fairness and good judgment, Israel Hatcher was appointed a Justice of the Peace, an office that allowed him to hold court to try minor violations of the law and to bind more serious cases over to the circuit court. Out of the 1,200 men in the jury pool, he was one of the twelve selected to try the case.

Serving on the jury for the Wynn and Tipton trial was something of a sacrifice for the Hatcher family. The distance from their home to Sevierville required a daylong horseback ride; the distance also meant Israel would have to stay at the county seat for the duration of the trial. Living as they did in an isolated area, there was the possibility that some White Cap members might raid their house while Mrs. Hatcher and the children were alone. But duty was not a strange word to Israel, and he knew the White Caps had to be laid to rest.

Four days were spent in selecting a jury, and the trial took two days. The day following closing arguments, the verdict was handed down: guilty of murder in the first degree. The judge pronounced the sentence of death by hanging. Ironically, on the night the trial began William Wynn, brother of Pleasant, accosted Sheriff Maples on a public street. The encounter ended with Maples killing Wynn in an act of self-defense. On the day sentence was pronounced against Pleasant Wynn, the funeral procession of William wound past the courthouse.

By this time the feeling against J. W. Catlett was very strong, so much so that his attorney appealed successfully for a change of venue; the trial was moved to Morristown, Tennessee. Both Pleas Wynn and Tipton testified against Catlett, saying he had talked with them about murdering the Whaleys and had paid Wynn to carry out the crime. However, Catlett's attorney attacked the credibility of the witnesses, and the trial ended in a hung jury.

One result of the trials was that Davis was elected sheriff in the 1898 election and would thus preside over the execution of two of the gang he had so long opposed.

On July 4, 1899, Wynn and Tipton began their final day of life. From their cell they could hear the sounds of hammers and saws as the gallows was constructed on the lawn of the courthouse.

A minister from one of the town's churches came to talk with the men, and Tipton stated that he wished to be baptized. Under heavy guard he was taken from the jail to the Pigeon River, just a block away, and the ceremony took place before a large crowd. As noon approached on July 5, every foot of space around the courthouse was packed with people. Suddenly Sheriff Davis appeared on the steps of the courthouse and announced that the men had been given an extra hour to be with their families. At 1:00 a solemn procession emerged from the jail and made its way to the gallows. Wynn and Tipton both said a few words to the hushed crowd, and then Sheriff Davis placed cloth hoods over their heads and the trap was sprung. Ironically, the last thing Tipton, who had been a carpenter, saw was the fence he had built around the courthouse lawn. Israel Hatcher was present in the crowd.

With the execution of Wynn and Tipton, the White Caps disappeared from Sevier County. Other things were claiming the attention of the nation and of the local population. In the summer of 1898, the Spanish-American War began, and a wave of patriotism swept over the countryside, making local and personal differences less important. Railroads began to be built into the Smoky Mountain area, bringing an improved economy and a sense of being more connected with a larger world. But across Sevier County a few lonely graves mark the final resting places of both White Caps members and their victims.

CHAPTER 4

Wicked Witch, Weary Woman, Misunderstood Mother?

The Legend of Nancy Dude

There can be no doubt that Nancy Kerlee [*sic*] was one of the most pronounced of these human freaks. Her very looks, her face and form, are the most eloquent and convincing arguments in support of the theory that she was a total and utter moral reprobate, that her degeneracy was complete both by heredity and personal training, that only half of her personality had been cultivated or allowed to develop by natural tendency, and that her moral self had steadily beaten the paths of least resistance. Her life stood shrouded by the mists of darkness and moral neglect.

—*From* A Serpent Slips into a Modern Eden
by James Turpin

This harsh assessment of Nancy Kerley reflects the legend that surrounds this tragic woman of the Smoky Mountains. Usually called Nancy Dude, she was a figure used to frighten children. Indeed, her name raised chill bumps on parents throughout the Smoky Mountains for generations.

To some people, Nancy Dude was a crazy old woman. She was not sociable but preferred her own company; she did not speak to her neighbors, did not take part in the activities of any church, and mumbled to herself. It was recognized in her community that she spent a great deal of time outdoors and was familiar with the herbs that grew in the mountains, so she was considered a "granny woman" who could provide folk medicine on request. But few dared ask Nancy Dude for help because some of the more superstitious of her neighbors said she was a witch and could cast spells that brought bad luck to those she cursed—their livestock died, their children got sick, their springs or wells dried up. Nancy Dude was a person to be feared and avoided.

The wisdom of avoiding Nancy was made obvious to all when, in 1913, the sixty-five-year-old woman was arrested on a charge of having murdered one of her grandchildren. She had allegedly walled two-year-old Roberta Ann Putnam into a crevice in the rocks on the side of a mountain and left her to die of hunger and cold. Such a thing was unthinkable, inhuman, and diabolical. The close-knit mountain families felt that this shocking incident only confirmed that all the terrible stories that had been told about Nancy Dude for so many years must be true. When the wheels of justice turned too slowly to suit the rattled locals, a mob tried to lynch her, but she was saved by law officers and stood before a judge. The sentence of thirty years she received was not nearly long enough to suit many. When Nancy Dude was sent off to the state prison, many said "good riddance."

Even today in the Smoky Mountains around Waynesville and Bryson City, North Carolina, people tell stories about Nancy Dude and discuss her saga. Who was Nancy Dude and just what did she do, and under what circumstances?

The legend depicts her as a reclusive, repellent, taciturn, mentally challenged, dangerous old woman who had no compunction in taking the life of an infant. Her history is somewhat more complicated.

In 1848 John and Kathleen Conard were living near Waynesville, North Carolina, on a small farm. That year their first child, Nancy Ann, was born. In due course there were other children and, as the oldest, Nancy was expected to help her mother take care of the younger ones. From her earliest days Nancy knew a life of hard work, but her life, and that of her family, was no harder than that of most other small mountain farmers.

The coming of the Civil War in 1861 changed life for Nancy and her family. The issues that tore the nation apart were not felt as strongly in the mountains as they were in other parts of North Carolina. Slavery, secession, and states' rights all meant little to the mountain people, who for the most part would have preferred to be left alone to get on with making a living. But the tentacles of war penetrated even the most remote valley in the Smoky Mountains. John Conard was drafted into the Confederate army and went away to fight. Some of his neighbors hid in the mountains to escape the draft, and some others sided with the Union.

With her father away, Nancy and her siblings had to work even harder to help their mother make their land produce most of the food they needed. Sugar and coffee became scarce as the blockade declared by the United States cut off trade with the Confederacy, but to the Conards these were luxuries; it was the absence of salt that affected them most. Without salt they could not cure and preserve meat to feed themselves during the warm months. A difficult life became even harder because of the war.

During the spring of 1865, as the war was coming to an end, Colonel Robert Kirk led a force of US soldiers into eastern Tennessee and western North Carolina to stamp out pockets of Confederate support. This raid left a lasting impression on Nancy as some of her neighbors were summarily executed on charges of being spies and a good deal of property was destroyed. John Conard returned from the war in May 1865, but his health was broken by diseases he had contracted while in the army, and he was never again able to perform the heavy physical labor required to make a small farm support a family. This began the downward spiral for Nancy that would continue for the rest of her life.

Even in hard times romances develop, and Nancy agreed to marry a neighbor, Howard Kerley, in April 1866. The new family worked, with the help of neighbors, to build a cabin for themselves and to clear land for a small farm while Howard continued to help his father farm the Kerleys' land. A son, William Henry Kerley, was born in December 1869. Not much is known of the life of this young couple. In general terms, life on any small farm was one of constant labor for both men and women because it took two people to raise a crop and do the necessary work of keeping house, cooking food, washing clothes, and preserving provisions for the winter. During the decades following the Civil War, money was in short supply throughout the South, so the Kerleys, like many other small farm families, ate what they grew and foraged from the surrounding countryside. A significant portion of their cash income was set aside to pay the property tax on their land. One telling feature is that Nancy had only one child during the sixteen years she and Howard were together; whether the cause was physical or the result of a lukewarm relationship will never be known. Nancy was deeply affected by the death of her father in 1882 and by the decision of her mother to move across the mountains to Tennessee, where she had relatives who would care for her.

What is known is that when William Henry was about thirteen years old, Nancy, after sixteen years of marriage, left her husband and son and moved into the house of Dude Hannah. Dude had a well-deserved reputation in the community as a bad character—albeit one with a charming side to his personality. He made his living by doing odd jobs for people in the community and had the talent to have developed into a skilled craftsman if he had so desired. Instead, Dude lived on the edge of financial survival and beyond the boundary of social respectability. What Nancy saw in Dude to make her leave her husband and son no one can now say, but the theme of "good girl attracted to bad boy" is an old one in literature and folklore. One of the old ballads still sung in the mountains is about a young wife and mother who runs away with Black Jack Davy. When her husband comes after her, the woman tells him:

Very well can I forsaken my house an' home
Very well can I forsaken my baby
Very well can I forsaken my own true one
An' go with the Black Jack Davy
An' go with the Black Jack Davy

This is just what Nancy did.

In the eyes of the community Nancy was now a total outcast. She had violated the social, moral, and religious norms of her community and was no longer considered a fit member of respectable society. This response to her actions only increased Nancy's habits of being taciturn and socially detached. Several months later, Nancy and Dude Hannah had a daughter, Elizabeth. While Nancy became a social pariah, Howard and William became the butt of jokes and the object of cutting comments for years to come.

Life with Dude was even more difficult than before. Dude did not work regularly, did not cultivate a crop, and was a binge drinker. When he was drinking Dude regularly became violently abusive and struck both Nancy and Elizabeth. Mother and daughter endured these conditions for several years, perhaps because they had nowhere else to go, until a disaster struck. In a drunken rage Dude threw a kerosene lamp against the wall of their cabin and the entire structure went up in flames. Nancy and Elizabeth escaped with only the clothes they were wearing, but this was the breaking point; they left Dude Hannah and went to the home of Joe and Jane Putnam.

The Putnams were sharecroppers on the farm of Mr. George Garrett. Sharecroppers, also called "tenant farmers," lived on the farm where they worked and, in return for their labor, kept a part of the crop they raised. The remainder of the crop went to the land-owner as a rent payment. Both Joe and Jane Putnam were in poor health and most of the work was done by their son, Will; therefore, Nancy and Elizabeth were welcome because they would provide additional labor.

Elizabeth and Will were both young people and were con-stantly in each other's company. In the isolated rural conditions in which they lived, the company of other people their age was rare, so it is not surprising that in 1910 Elizabeth became pregnant and broached the subject of marriage to Will. The union was made offi-cial and a daughter, Roberta Ann, was born long enough after the wedding that gossip was held to a minimum. The baby had blond hair and developed a cheerful personality, though her life was chal-lenging, even when she was an infant. Three years after her birth, economic problems were overwhelming the household.

Nancy was sixty-five years old, an old person by the standards of the day when the average life expectancy was about sixty-seven. She could no longer do as much work as she once had. The small cabin where they lived was crowded, and another child was on the way. Will could not wrest enough food and money from their share of the crop they produced, so a difficult decision was made.

In 1913 Nancy, Elizabeth, and Roberta Ann left their home and went across the Smoky Mountain peaks to live with relatives of Nancy's mother in Hartford, Tennessee. The economic situation in Tennessee proved to be just as difficult as in North Carolina, so the three returned to their home.

Why Will Putnam continued to be a sharecropper is some-thing of a mystery. The opening years of the twentieth century saw the mountains enjoy a degree of prosperity. Commercial logging had come to the Smokies in the 1890s, and there were jobs to be had, with regular pay, from a number of timber companies. Mining for copper and other minerals was a small-scale industry in North Carolina, and the prices paid for agricultural products were rising. It would seem that Will and Elizabeth Putnam might have found an opportunity to improve their economic situation, but they did not.

By February 1913, food was running low. The supplies laid in the previous autumn were nigh exhausted, and it was clear there would not be enough food to last until spring brought the opportunity to grow and to forage for more. Nancy's relatives in Tennessee were not able to provide relief, and Will had no family in North Carolina. Somehow the family reached a heart-wrenching conclusion: Roberta Ann would have to be sent away. This was not the only family being forced to such a conclusion. In the early twentieth century sending children to relatives or placing them as wards of the state happened with distressing frequency.

Each county in most states maintained a "county poor farm" where indigent elderly people could find a room and board in return for whatever work they could do. These county homes seldom took children, especially toddlers, but placing Roberta Ann in the county home was one option. Another was to get in touch with some kindhearted person who would take her into their family, even if she was not formally adopted.

February 26, 1913, was remembered as a typically cold mountain day. That morning Nancy, accompanied by Roberta Ann, left the cabin where they lived and set off on foot over Utah Mountain, seeking someplace to care for the child. Late that afternoon Nancy returned home alone, and here the mystery and legend become tangled.

Nancy told Will and Elizabeth that she had met "a man in a buggy" and that he ran a home for children whose families could not care for them. After some conversation this man had agreed to give Roberta Ann a home; she was last seen as the buggy drove off along the rough mountain road. Will and Elizabeth did not ask any questions.

As the days passed, neighbors began to ask why they had not seen Roberta Ann. Some of these neighbors were not satisfied with the terse answers given by Nancy and the other family members, so they asked Deputy Sheriff Jack Carver to look into the matter. The fact that the neighbors were inquisitive and became suspicious enough to go the authorities reveals something about the standing Nancy and the Putnams had in the community. The fact that the deputy sheriff undertook an investigation says even more.

Carver soon identified the "man in a buggy" as the Reverend W. T. Fincher. The preacher told Carver that he had indeed met Nancy and Roberta Ann on February 26 and had given them a ride in his buggy. Nothing had been discussed about Roberta Ann, and Nancy had asked to get out at a fork in the road. That was the last Reverend Fincher had seen of them. This testimony raised suspicions in the neighborhood to the extent that Nancy was arrested on a charge of suspicion of murder while Will and Elizabeth were arrested as possible accomplices. This was rather thin evidence, but the fact that an arrest was made on such a basis again reveals the apparent attitude that Nancy was not a good member of society;

her past with Dude Hannah still haunted her and was now working to destroy her.

Deputy Sheriff Carver knew he had to have better evidence against Nancy if his case was to stand up in court. Using the strong feelings in the community, Carver organized a search party to try to discover the remains of Roberta Ann. Although it was early spring, and farmwork needed to be done to get ready for the coming year, a very large party turned out to search the wooded slopes of the mountain where Roberta Ann was last reported to have been seen by Reverend Fincher. On the fourth day of the search, a young man, Frank James, followed his dog who had found a scent. The trail led to a rock face where a crevice in the rock had been walled up with large slabs of stone. Pulling a few of the smaller pieces of stone away, Frank James saw the remains of a young child.

Frank's cries for help soon brought several of the searchers to his side, and they tore down the rock wall. Some of the stones were so large that two men were required to move them. Behind the barrier they found all that was left of Roberta Ann. Nancy was immediately charged with murder in the first degree while Will and Elizabeth were released. In the minds of the local residents, Nancy was a wicked woman, a witch in attitude, and it was self-evident to them that she was guilty of heartless cruelty in walling up her granddaughter and leaving the toddler to die of cold and starvation.

Nancy was held for trial in the county jail at Waynesville, North Carolina, and when the next session of court convened, seventy-five local men were called for jury duty. After questioning, Judge Garland S. Ferguson ruled that none of the prospective jurors could be seated because all of them had expressed the opinion that

Nancy was guilty. The announcement by the judge that an unbiased jury could not be seated caused a riot. Men swarmed toward the judge's bench in an attempt to seize the accused and lynch her. Only swift action and drawn guns by the police present saved Nancy's life.

A change of venue took the case to Bryson City, and there Nancy had to wait for the next session of court to convene. By the time a year had passed, the attorney who had been appointed to defend Nancy, S. A. Black, was convinced that a fair trial was not possible anywhere in the area. Attempting to save his client's life, Mr. Black convinced Nancy to plead guilty to murder in the second degree. As a result, she was sentenced to thirty years in prison without a jury ever having evaluated the evidence against her.

With Nancy now out of sight, locked away for what most people thought would be the rest of her life, interest in Roberta Ann's case slowly died away. Will and Elizabeth Putnam got on with their lives as best they could, as did Howard and William Henry Kerley. Then, on May 21, 1929, the governor of North Carolina ordered Nancy released because of her advanced age—she was eighty years old.

William Henry Kerley agreed to let his mother live out the rest of her days with him. Apparently, he held no grudge against her for walking out on him when he was just thirteen, nor did he think her a wicked witch. Rather, he seemed to have seen her as a weary woman, worn down by the hard work needed to make a living in the mountains. Or, perhaps, he thought she was a misunderstood mother who had not always made good decisions but who had always loved her children in her own way.

At any rate, hard work and poverty continued to be Nancy's lot. The house she and her son occupied did not have running water or electricity. Money was scarce, and both Nancy and William had to struggle to find enough food to sustain them. When the Great Smoky Mountains National Park opened, Nancy found an additional source of income: she chopped firewood and sold it to campers visiting the Deep Creek section of the park at Bryson City. She was engaged in that activity when she fell dead of a heart attack on September 12, 1952. She was 104 years old.

The legend of Nancy Dude still stirs discussion and controversy among those who know her story. Some argue that Nancy was innocent of murder, and that she loved her children and grandchildren, even though she was taciturn and not outwardly affectionate. These supporters point out that a jury never heard and evaluated the evidence against Nancy, and that her conviction was a plea bargain she might have made to protect the actual perpetrator of the crime. They especially point to the size of the rocks used to close up the crevice where the body of Roberta Ann was found—rocks that took two men to move. Could an elderly woman who weighed less than eighty pounds have moved such stones?

There is a ballad, "Poor Child," that relates the tale of Nancy Dude, and Smoky Mountain playwright Gary Carden wrote a play that tells her story, based on the book *The Legend of Nancy Dude* by Maurice Stanley. Carden's play presents Nancy as a weary and misunderstood woman who was ostracized by her community for abandoning her family and having a child out of wedlock with another man.

No matter how one views her, Nancy Dude is an enduring character in Smoky Mountain myths and legends.

CHAPTER 5

Mythical Moonshine

Legendary "Likker" to Legal Libation

Myth and legend surround one product indelibly fixed in popular imagination with the Smoky Mountains— moonshine, the popular name for illegally produced, untaxed, un-aged whiskey. Moonshine and the people who make it, moonshiners, are stock figures in popular culture's view of mountain people and mountain life. From the comic strip character Snuffy Smith to the cult movie *Thunder Road* to television programs such as *The Beverly Hillbillies*, moonshine and mountains always go together. Distilling was part of frontier life and, before the Civil War, was a common practice not only in the Appalachian area but all along the frontier. While many states have a history of moonshine, the traditions associated with it are centered in the Great Smoky Mountains where a respect for the craft of distilling developed, and the folklore and traditions surrounding it were kept alive.

Some of the characters associated with the making of moonshine possess legendary qualities. Lewis Redmond was the first mythic moonshiner, becoming both an outlaw and a protector of people in the vicinity of Bryson City, North Carolina, a nineteenth-century Smoky Mountains "Robin Hood."

Redmond was born around 1854 and gave the place of his birth variously as north Georgia and western North Carolina. During the Civil War he was living in the area near Bryson City and often visited the camp of soldiers of the Thomas Legion, a Confederate unit composed of Cherokee and mountaineers. The soldiers gave Redmond the nickname "Major," and he later used this as a title.

The Redmond family was left destitute by the aftermath of the Civil War, as was nearly the entire South. Before the war, making whiskey was an untaxed, entirely legal activity; most small farmers in remote locations made liquor to preserve part of their crop by rendering corn and fruit into a commodity that did not spoil. If the individual farmer did not have a small still to make whiskey from corn or brandy from fruit, there was usually someone in the community who would perform the work in exchange for part of the product. During the Civil War the United States placed an excise tax of twenty cents a gallon on whiskey, a tax that rose to two dollars a gallon by 1865. Until the end of the conflict, this tax did not affect the residents of the Smoky Mountains since they were part of the Confederacy. The end of the war brought enforcement of the law, and the high tax meant that a small farmer producing only a few gallons of whiskey paid more in tax than he realized in profit. Once making and selling untaxed whiskey became illegal, moonshining

This typical small still is a display at the Oconoluftee Visitor Center in the Great Smoky Mountains National Park.

was born, so called because the distiller made whiskey at night when the smoke from the still could not be seen. The mountain people did not use the term "moonshine," but kept a term left over from the war years. The United States had proclaimed a blockade of the Confederacy to prevent essential goods from reaching the South, so the mountain people called making untaxed whiskey "blockading" and the product was "blockade." To those who had supported the Confederacy, the tax on whiskey seemed another attack on states' rights; to those who had supported the Union, the tax was an unfair burden they did not deserve. As a boy not even in his teens, Redmond was part of this controversy because his family, like many others, simply ignored the law and kept on making small amounts of whiskey to sell.

By the time Redmond was twenty-two years old he was making whiskey himself as well as purchasing it from neighbors, and exporting the illegal product to cities outside the mountains. According to the legend, if a man from whom Redmond purchased whiskey was arrested, the wife and family of the man regularly found food on their doorstep, their property taxes were paid by an unknown person, and no harm came to them until the man of the family was released from prison.

In 1876 a US deputy marshal was shot and killed by Redmond when he attempted to arrest him. Redmond fled to Pickens County, South Carolina, just across the state line, and was soon involved with other men who made that mountainous area a hotbed of anti-government activity. When he was finally arrested, Redmond escaped and raised a gang of men who raided the home of the officer who had arrested him, forcing the officer to return Redmond's horse, money, and whiskey he had seized.

By 1879 Redmond was back in the area of Bryson City, where he reorganized his network of moonshiners and resumed his business of making and selling whiskey. According to one story, he was arrested and taken to the jail in Bryson City. On a visit his wife brought him his favorite pillow "to help him sleep better." The pillow contained a pistol, which he used to escape yet again. Of course, his Robin Hood–esque acts of charity continued to win him the support and affection of many citizens, or so says the myth. In 1881 the law caught up with Redmond; he was wounded in a raid on his home, arrested, and taken back to South Carolina for trial. On August 29, 1881, Redmond was sentenced to ten years in federal prison. Thirty months later Redmond was pardoned by President Chester A. Arthur. Redmond returned to his old haunts, got a job in a legal distillery, and died in 1906. His wife lived until 1933.

During his life, Redmond became a mysterious, romantic figure with a national reputation thanks to journalists and writers. Appalachia became characterized as a mysterious place full of lawlessness and depravity, in contrast to the perceived intellectual, cultural, and social superiority of people in the Northeast and urban centers of the Midwest. Fictitious and exaggerated accounts of life in the mountains became popular, and mountain people were often depicted as in need of "civilizing."

This view was not restricted to people from the North. Mary Noailles Murfree, a local-color writer from Murfreesboro, Tennessee, spent her summers at Montvale Springs in the Smoky Mountains. Her stories, set in the Smoky Mountains, depict the mountain people as lazy, drunken degenerates. Such stories not only produced a fascination with the mountains, they also provided ammunition for "reformers" who felt compelled to make the local people "normal" and "modern."

The trial of legendary moonshiner Lewis Redmond took place in this building, the courthouse of Bryson City.

This attitude also made the readers of such material subject to manipulation by mountaineers who were shrewd enough to use this simplistic approach for their own purposes. Redmond provides a good example of a moonshiner doing just that. A journalist with the Charleston, South Carolina, *News and Courier* interviewed Redmond in the summer of 1878. Edward B. Crittenden, a bishop of the Methodist Episcopal Church, South, wrote a romantic and highly inaccurate account of Redmond's life in 1892 based on a personal interview with Redmond. In the 1890s Redmond gave an interview to yet another writer. In each of these three accounts, Redmond gives a different date and place for his birth, admits to having killed several men but always because he had no choice, claims to have been a protector of helpless women and children who were victims of corrupt government agencies, and said he rescued at least one pure, innocent young woman from the hands of an angry mob.

Across the mountains from Bryson City is Cades Cove, today one of the must-see spots for visitors to the Great Smoky Mountains National Park. In the years after the Civil War, the Chestnut Flats area of Cades Cove was a center of moonshining, the result of water that is almost entirely free of minerals that would negatively affect the taste of whiskey. In 1878 US Deputy Elias Cooper raided a still in Chestnut Flats. He and the accompanying party of law officers were making their way to Maryville when they were ambushed by moonshiners. Over forty shots were exchanged but, fortunately, no fatalities resulted.

The churches of Cades Cove—the Primitive Baptists and the Methodists—were opposed to the use of alcohol as a beverage, but both took a tolerant view of the farmer who made a few gallons of whiskey or fruit brandy as part of his diversified economic activity. And no notice was taken of the occasional use of alcohol for medicinal purposes; after all, there was no other locally available painkiller for headaches and rheumatism, or good medicine for coughs. Even so, the making of whiskey split the Cades Cove community at times. John Walter Oliver was a minister of the Primitive Baptist Church and postman for Cades Cove, delivering the mail to the families in the valley. His beliefs made him opposed to moonshine and his position as postman allowed him to travel regularly and to be quite familiar with the location of every house in the area. Sighting smoke at a place he knew held no house was an indication of a still, and Oliver often reported these locations to the authorities. Josiah Gregory owned a still that was raided and destroyed; in retaliation, he paid two young men to burn two barns belonging to Oliver.

Horace Kephart, the writer who helped popularize the idea of a national park in the Smoky Mountains, was so enamored of the legends and picturesque characters surrounding moonshining that he devoted seven of the twenty chapters of his book on the mountains to the subject.

The romanticized view of making untaxed whiskey took a turn in a new direction in the twentieth century. North Carolina and Tennessee voted to become "dry" states early in the century, and national prohibition on the manufacturing, distribution, and sales of all alcohol beverages went into effect as part of the effort to provide more food for soldiers fighting in World War I. The elimination of legal whiskey raised the profits to be made from illegal whiskey to as much as $6.00 a gallon and created a national market for what had been largely a local and regional drink. Prohibition coincided with state and national programs to build better roads and the mass production of automobiles and trucks. Organized crime syndicates in large cities made alliances with moonshiners in the mountains to begin producing large amounts of whiskey and to transport it to urban markets. Making whiskey ceased being a cottage craft and became a large industry. Seemingly innocent farmers driving innocuous loads of farm produce to the county seat, with a few gallons of whiskey hidden under a load of apples, were replaced by young men who modified automobiles to carry several hundred gallons of whiskey, the cars powered by rebuilt engines capable of much higher speeds. Men such as Dick Denton, Ike Costner, and Robert Gunter came to dominate Smoky Mountain moonshining. Instead of 40-gallon copper stills, whiskey-making operations used 1,000- and 1,500-gallon stills heated by steam. Ike Coster even built an airstrip in what is now the Cosby area of the Great Smoky Mountains National Park and flew whiskey to Chicago.

Some of the young men who drove the fast cars to deliver whiskey began to make a sport of racing each other when they were not running whiskey, thus birthing the sport we now associate with the National Association of Stock Car Auto Racing, or NASCAR. The combination of fast cars, reckless young men, and illegal whiskey gave birth to yet another romanticized vision of life in the mountains in the movie *Thunder Road*, starring Robert Mitchum, who also directed the film.

An icon of both moonshining and NASCAR was Junior Johnson, named for his father, Robert Glenn Johnson Sr., and who became such a folk hero that the writer Tom Wolfe wrote an article in *Esquire* naming Junior Johnson as "the last great American Hero." Junior Johnson began driving in the fields and along the dirt roads near his North Carolina home when he was ten or eleven years old, and by the time he was fourteen he was an expert driver. With these skills he soon was running whiskey for his father, who was a well-known moonshiner. Junior accepted the romanticized view that making whiskey was a necessary economic activity; he once said, "Where I lived, if you didn't make whiskey you didn't have bread to put on the table. My dad had ten other families he provided for."

Driving fast was essential for Junior Johnson and the other "whiskey car" drivers. "Lose at the race track and you go home, lose with a load of 'shine and you go to jail," he commented on one occasion. Beginning with the favorite car of whiskey runners, a 1940 Ford Coupe with a flathead V-8 cylinder engine, the drivers and their mechanics began to make modifications to the engines to make the cars faster and to the suspension to make the cars more stable in making turns. Johnson recalled, "I adapted a lot of the technology from my liquor cars to my race cars and won a lot of races that way." Government agents never caught Johnson in a car chase, but he was arrested while helping his father run their still. Johnson eventually left the moonshine business and became a famous NASCAR driver and a successful businessman.

The idyllic view of moonshine continues in the twenty-first century. In 1999 Marvin "Popcorn" Sutton of Maggie Valley on the North Carolina side of the Smoky Mountains self-published a book about his escapades as a whiskey maker. This book caught the attention of documentarian Neal Hutchison, who made a film about Sutton, *The Last One.* This documentary film reached a wide audience on public broadcasting channels and led to a feature shown on the History Channel, *Hillbilly: The Real Story.* Sutton played the stereotypical role to the hilt, giving the audience just what it wanted to suit its preconceived ideas. He portrayed a character who always wore overalls, a flannel shirt, and a floppy hat, and who drove a rattletrap vehicle. Sutton was another of those shrewd mountaineers who saw what tourists wanted and happily gave it to them, for a price. Unfortunately, success made Sutton greedy and he began making moonshine to sell to those who came to see him. He was arrested in 2008 and committed suicide rather than face prison.

What was this legendary "likker," and how was it produced? Many of the Scotch-Irish and Scots settlers in the Smoky Mountain area brought stills with them. The Celtic lands are the home of distilling, and many useful household products are produced by distilling, not just alcohol. In America one adjustment to the practice of distilling was made in short order: Indian corn was substituted for rye, barley, or wheat as the grain being distilled. Corn is a crop readily grown in abundance.

The first step in production is to place whole kernels of corn in warm water and allow them to sprout. When the sprouts are over an inch in length, the kernels are then ground coarsely at a mill. The ground kernels are mixed with cornmeal, and hot water is added to make mash. This mixture is allowed to stand for up to ten days while fermentation takes place. At the end of that time the mash has an alcohol content of about 10 percent and is ready to distill.

The mash is placed in a still pot, preferably made of copper, and a fire is built under the pot to bring the mash to a boil at 173 degrees Fahrenheit. The steam from the boiling mash escapes through a copper tube, which is wound into a coil and is called a "worm." As the steam cools in the worm, it condenses to liquid and is caught in a container as it drips from the worm. The condensation process can be sped up by running part of the tube leading from the worm through a barrel of cool water.

The first run of the mash is traditionally called "singlings" and is not fit to drink because of the amount of fusel oil present. The still pot has to be thoroughly cleaned after making the singlings, and the liquid has to be distilled a second time. As the liquid leaves the worm on the second run, it is usual for it to be filtered through a cloth sack filled with ground charcoal. The second run is ready for immediate consumption. Aquila "Quil" Rose was a well-known moonshiner interviewed by Kephart. Rose stated, "A slick-faced dude from Knoxville told me once that all good red liquor was aged and that if I'd age my blockade it would bring a fancy price. Well, Sir, I tried it; I kept some for three months—and by godlings, it ain't so!"

Turning corn into whiskey was good economics. A bushel of corn, for much of the nineteenth century, sold for twenty-five cents, yet this same bushel of corn would produce two and a half gallons of whiskey, which sold for $1.25. A bushel of corn weighs fifty-five pounds, while two-and-a-half gallons of whiskey weighs about twenty-two pounds; thus, a farmer who used part of his corn crop to make whiskey increased the value of his commodity through the added labor and he addressed the problem of taking a heavy load to market via bad roads by reducing the weight of the commodity. Also, if for any reason a farmer could not get his corn to market the corn would rot, but if he turned the corn into whiskey it would keep for an indefinite period and would actually increase in value over time. Finally, frugal farmers knew that pigs grew fat on the spent mash, so nothing was wasted in turning corn into whiskey.

There is no danger that mysterious moonshine will become a thing of the past; indeed, it has become very much a fixture in the contemporary life of the Smoky Mountains. This "legendary likker" has become a legal libation. The end of national prohibition in 1933 lessened the demand for moonshine nationally, though state and local "dry" laws guaranteed there was still a market for untaxed whiskey. The repeal of these laws in the last part of the twentieth century more or less finished off the demand for moonshine, and it seemed, for a moment, that homemade whiskey would become merely a matter of folklore. For over a century Tennessee had on the books a law limiting legal distilling to three counties where the nearly mineral-free water enhances the taste of whiskey: Moore (the home of Jack Daniel's), Coffee (the home of George Dickel), and Lincoln (the home of Pritchard's rum).

In 2009 the Tennessee legislature made distilling legal throughout the state. North Carolina had passed a similar law in 2005.

The passage of the law that made distilling legal statewide had an immediate impression on Joe Baker, a criminal lawyer in Knoxville. As a native of the East Tennessee hills, Baker was familiar with the myths and legends surrounding the production of moonshine, and he came from a family that had once produced homemade whiskey. Baker contacted two friends from his college days, also attorneys, and the three obtained the first distiller's license issued by the state of Tennessee and opened a distillery using a two-hundred-year-old recipe handed down in Baker's family.

Although operating legally, this first moonshine still to operate openly in almost a century and a half faced some of the same problems their outlaw predecessors faced. One of these was securing proper containers. The traditional container for moonshine was quart Mason jars, usually used to preserve food. The law requires whiskey to be sold not by the quart, but in .750 milliliter containers, the modern version of the traditional "fifth of whiskey." Securing the proper-size jars required negotiations with the glass industry.

Baker and his partners decided to support the local economy as much as possible, so all the corn used at the distillery was, and is, purchased locally, as was, and is, the fruit used to flavor some of the varieties produced.

Since ten million people visit the Great Smoky Mountains in any given year, an appeal to the tourist industry was an obvious strategy for success, so the distillery was located on the main street of Gatlinburg. Today hundreds of people a day visit what was once carefully hidden: a moonshine still. The legendary "likker" has become a legal libation. Although, one wonders, since the distiller pays tax on the whiskey, is it really moonshine?

CHAPTER 6

The Legend of Paul Bunyan,
Smokies Style

A visitor to the great North Woods will soon encounter the story of Paul Bunyan, the legendary woodsman who could clear forty acres with a single swipe of his giant axe and then pull the logs out of the woods with his fabulous beast, Babe the Blue Ox. In Bemidji, Minnesota, there stands a pair of statues of Paul and Babe. In four other places, from Maine to California and Oregon, there are additional statues commemorating the figure who has come to represent the woodsmen who cleared the forests of the northern states.

A visitor to the Great Smoky Mountains National Park soon becomes aware that the mountains once were covered by vast swaths of virgin timber. The remaining pockets of those trees are one of the important features of the park. But, if the area was once a virgin forest and only a few pockets of old-growth timber now remain, the mountains must once have been the site of extensive logging. Who cut the timber from the Great Smoky Mountains?

Why is there no statue or memorial to those who were the Paul Bunyans of the Smokies? One answer is that the reality of the woodsman is quite different from the legend. What was the reality?

Part of the reality of the timber-cutting woodsmen were men who wore business suits, stiff white collars, and ties. These were the heads of companies who had money to invest in purchasing land and logging equipment, building railroads, and meeting all the other expenses of running a major business. Not exactly a fit for the Paul Bunyan legend, but a very much a part of the reality.

Since the days of early settlement, local settlers cut selected trees from locations close to streams, trimmed the limbs, sawed the logs into sixteen-foot sections, and floated the logs to market in times of high water. Small sawmills at Sevierville, Knoxville, and other burgeoning towns produced lumber for the local market, but this sort of logging made no real impact on the forests since it was a part-time occupation for a few families. The first business-man to come to the Smoky Mountains looking for timber was Jack Coburn, who moved from Michigan, where the forests were already being depleted, to the Hazel Creek area of North Carolina in 1888. Coburn was somewhat unusual for a logging company executive—he had gotten his start as a "timber cruiser," a man who roamed the woods looking at trees and deciding if they contained enough board feet of lumber to justify their purchase. A "board foot" is one foot long, one foot wide, and one inch thick, and is a standard measure in the lumber business in the United States and Canada.

Around 1890, Coburn began to purchase timber rights along Hazel Creek and its major tributaries. Purchasing timber rights meant Coburn bought the right to cut the trees on the property but the original owner retained title to the land. Logging began soon after 1890, when Coburn sold his timber rights to the Taylor and Crate Lumber Company of Buffalo, New York. Since the timber rights Coburn sold the company were along Hazel Creek and its tributaries, the trees were felled, trimmed of limbs, cut into sections, and floated down the mountain streams to the Little Tennessee River, where they were chained together into rafts and towed by steamboats downstream about 150 miles to a mill near Chattanooga, Tennessee. About the same time, Horace Ayers and William Ashe, employees of the US Forestry Service, surveyed the area and reported that there was an abundance of valuable timber and that the land could be purchased cheaply.

This "Paul Bunyan" activity did not last long; soon all the old trees conveniently located near streams had been cut, and Taylor and Crate moved on. Other methods of getting trees out of the woods and to mills were being developed. The W. M. Ritter Lumber Company of Columbus, Ohio, began purchasing timber rights and outright ownership of land in the Hazel Creek area in 1902–1903. Ritter was the largest lumber company in the United States and made much of its money by cutting hardwoods that were milled into flooring for upscale homes. Most of the trees Ritter would cut were on land to which they held the timber rights, but the company did purchase outright land for the construction of a railroad, sawmills, planing mills, drying kilns, and a townsite where the company built housing for one thousand workers. (The story of this town is told in the chapter "Ghost Towns Beneath Your Feet.") W. M. Ritter, and other company executives, did pay regular visits to the Hazel Creek area, and they were important parts of the lumbering activity, but they never swung an axe.

At almost the same time that Ritter Lumber Company was setting up operations in Hazel Creek, the Little River Lumber Company was moving into Tuckaleechee Cove on the Tennessee side of the mountains. A business associate of W. B. Townsend, John W. Fisher, owned a tannery in Walland, Tennessee. The tannery used a huge amount of bark to get the tannins that were used to process animal hides into leather. Fisher invited Townsend to begin logging operations in the Smoky Mountains, promising to purchase the bark. The Little River Lumber Company was formed by Townsend and Fisher, both of whom were from Pennsylvania, and they saw that the only feasible way to get lumber to market was to build a railroad. They built the Little River Railroad from Walland, Tennessee, where the Southern Railroad had a line that connected to Knoxville, to what would become the headquarters of the logging operations in Tuckaleechee Cove, a village that was named Townsend. The company initially purchased 40,000 acres of timber, then eventually purchased 40,000 more.

Most logging companies built narrow-gauge lines, which had rails thirty-six inches or less apart. These were cheaper to build than standard-gauge railroads, which had rails placed four feet, eight and one-half inches apart. This meant that a narrow-gauge railcar could not run on a standard-gauge line, and vice versa. W. B. Townsend, however, had the Little River Railroad constructed to standard gauge so his company did not have to transfer goods from one railcar to another when they reached the main rail line, thus saving time and expense; this also means railcars from the main lines could

Railway engine and logging crane used by Little River Lumber Company

run directly to Townsend. A small town soon grew up at Townsend with sawmills, planing mills, and facilities to dry lumber before loading it on railcars to be sent all over the United States to market.

Within a few months, the same train that took lumber to Knoxville was bringing back sportsmen and outdoors enthusiasts who wanted to fish, hunt, camp, and hike in the mountains.

None of the businessmen from any of the lumber companies were local people; all came from northern cities. This was true not only in the Smoky Mountains, but in nearly all areas that produced natural resources. The local economy got jobs as long as the resources lasted, but the profits went elsewhere.

The businessmen did not look like Paul Bunyan, nor did their equipment bear any resemblance at all to Babe the Blue Ox. Several methods were used to get the logs out of the woods, all of them destructive to the environment. If streams of sufficient size were available, "splash dams" would be built on the main stream and its tributaries. These dams, often constructed of wood, stopped most of the flow in a stream, allowing a large pool of water to accumulate behind the dam. While the water was pooling, logs would be hauled to the streambeds. When enough logs had been accumulated and enough water was pooled behind the dams, the water would be released in a controlled fashion so that the dams farthest upstream would be breached and, as the water reached the next downstream it would be breached, and so on down the stream. This meant that on the major watercourse a strong flood of water would crash along the streambed, filled with logs churning and tumbling in the current. While some logs snagged along the banks, the majority made the trip to the holding pond where logs were held until being taken to the sawmill. Obviously, this rush of water scoured the streambed, destroying habitat for all aquatic life, and flushed most of the fish downstream. This method of moving trees to sawmills was used on both the North Carolina and Tennessee sides of the Smoky Mountains.

Skidders were used in many areas of the Smoky Mountains. These were basically a steam-powered winch with a cable run uphill for as much as a mile (or sometimes more). Logs were attached to the cable, and the logs were dragged downhill. Of course, all vegetation in the path of the log was destroyed and the ground was plowed up, making erosion likely the next wet season. In very steep terrain the cable for the skidder might be run high aboveground to a tower and the logs hung from the cable for the descent. This avoided snagging logs in very steep places and was also less destructive to the forest.

The most important machine in getting logs out of the woods was the locomotive, which pulled the flatcars loaded with freshly cut timber to the mills. Most steam-powered locomotives are powered by drive rods, which work pistons that, in turn, transfer energy to the trucks (sets of wheels) that pull the locomotive over the tracks. Such rod-driven engines have strict limits as to the steepness of the grade they can negotiate and they have a wide turning radius. Merely looking at a railroad track shows how the line of rails is engineered to lessen grades and provide sweeping turns. These limitations meant traditional locomotives would not work well in the Smoky Mountains, where steep grades are unavoidable and tight curves are necessary.

Ephraim Shay, a lumberman from Michigan, solved this problem by inventing a new design for locomotives. Beginning in 1873, Shay experimented with a design that placed the water tank on the left side of the locomotive and then placed a boiler over each set of trucks on the right side. The pistons ran vertically from the boiler down to the gears that drove each truck. This change in design produced so much additional driving power that rails could be laid on the ground, no roadbed was necessary, and the engine could pull a set of fully loaded railcars up a grade of one foot of rise for each seven-foot-long distance. Also, the engines could negotiate curves with a radius of fifty to one hundred feet, much tighter than any other engine. Shay sold his patents for the engines to the Lima Locomotive Works in Lima, Ohio, and they became widely used by many logging companies, including the Little River Lumber Company.

The Baldwin engines were powered in the traditional way and were popular with logging companies in the Smoky Mountains for moving railcars on the fringes of the mountains where the terrain was less challenging. The Baldwin engines could travel faster than the powerful, but more nimble, Shay engines.

Any machine needs to be maintained; while some men worked driving the engines and loading the logs onto the railcars, other men worked to keep the boilers of the steam engines filled with water, loaded the tenders with coal to fuel the firebox under the boiler, cleaned out the ash from the firebox so the fuel would burn clean, oiled the moving parts, and swept out the cab where the engineer and fireman worked. One maintenance job now almost forgotten was the task of filling hoppers with bushel after bushel of dry sand. Smooth steel wheels running on smooth steel rails need something to grip for traction, and sand provided that grip. Hoppers were built into the engines ahead of each truck, and the engineer was able to control the flow of sand onto the rails from his position in the cab. If the sand got wet, clogging the outlet from the hopper to the rails, the train would not be able to pull its load uphill; worse, if the sand failed going downhill, gravity would take over and the train would become a runaway. The Little River Railroad lost two engines in one day in April 1931 along Marks Creek when engines No. 9 and No. 11 ran away. If no lives had been lost (the first accident claimed two victims), these accidents might have appeared somewhat comical. A Ritter Company locomotive ran off the track and landed upside down in Hazel Creek. Charlie Wilson had been the engineer on the train and had escaped unharmed. As a company executive stood on the banks of the creek bemoaning the cost of retrieving and repairing the engine, Wilson coolly observed, "Well, they is a dozen cans of Prince Albert pipe tobacco underwater that I jest got from the commissary this morning."

While the echoes of steam train whistles have long since faded from memory for most people, those visiting the Great Smoky Mountains National Park today may find themselves walking along a trail with an easy grade, passing rocks with holes drilled into them, and, if they are sharp-eyed, seeing occasional scraps of metal. These trails, such as the Little River Trail at Elkmont, follow the roadbeds of the old logging railroads. The motor road from Townsend, Tennessee, to Elkmont Campground also follows the route once used by the railroad.

Money and machinery did not fell trees and cut them into logs; this was done by human hands—flesh-and-blood versions of Paul Bunyan. The first group of workers, "swampers," had the job of clearing away all brush and undergrowth to make clear pathways to the stands of big trees. Percheron horses were often used to drag logs along these cleared paths until they could be loaded on railcars. If the logs were not enormous, teams of four to six mules would be used instead of horses. A second set of crews built wooden flumes, V-shaped troughs in which logs could be placed and dragged down the mountain. Finally came the men with crosscut saws and axes, known in the Smokies as "woodhicks."

Crosscut saws had a handle at each end; two team members each took a handle and the two began to work in rhythm, pulling the saw back and forth through the trunk of the tree. The saws came in two lengths, eight and eleven feet. Some of the trees being felled were so thick that one handle had to be removed to pull the saw through the cut. A three-man crew was expected to cut 10,000 board feet per day, which involved cutting out the tops, removing the limbs, and cutting the trunks into sixteen-foot sections. This meant felling ten to twelve trees each day, with each tree being 24 to 30 inches in diameter. One logger, in later years, told an interviewer that "if you had a sharp saw and a buddy at the other end who knew what he was doing the work wasn't too much; but if you had a bad worker or one who didn't know what he was doing, you could get killed in a minute."

The workday was ten to twelve hours a day, six days a week, for pay ranging from seven to twelve cents per hour. Even so, this was more money than could be earned annually from small subsistence farms. The Ritter Lumber Company paid in cash, not company scrip, therefore their workers could maximize their income by shopping for bargains at any available store instead of being limited to the "company store." However, the Little River Lumber Company paid in company scrip, which the workers called "doogaloo."

One worker recalled that the families seldom had any cash, but used their salaries to purchase groceries and overalls.

These Smoky Mountain Paul Bunyans did not come into the woods alone. Many of the workers were married and brought their wives and children with them to the logging camps. Since the camps had to be moved often to keep the men near to the trees being cut, the lumber companies furnished housing. A common type was called a "set off house" because it was about twelve by twelve feet, made of lightweight lumber and tar paper, and had a hook permanently fixed to its ridgepole so it could be set on a flatcar at one location and set off at the new campsite. At the headquarters sites, where the mills were located, the companies provided more substantial housing.

The logging camps often had schools, churches, stores, and other basic facilities. However, they were isolated and were surrounded by acres and acres of drying treetops, limbs, brush piles, and other readily combustible material. With logging operations depending on the use of steam-powered machinery, sparks from smokestacks presented a constant fire danger. In 1917 fire threatened Higdon, a logging camp not far from the present location of the Tremont Environmental Center. All who wished to leave the area were given rides to safety on the Little River Railroad, but Dorie Cope, along with her husband and parents, stayed to fight the fire.

The two men of the family worked in the woods while the two women ran a boardinghouse, providing two meals a day for eight unmarried men. All eight of the boarders stayed to help fight the fire.

The people who stayed to fight the fire got all the containers available and formed a bucket brigade from the river to the camp. They doused each house in turn, over and over, all through the night. Before dawn the wind changed directions and blew the flames back onto already charred areas. By that time, only three houses still stood in Higdon. Ironically, the family living in one of them had placed all their possessions on rocks in the river. Flying debris had burned all their household goods while their empty house stood untouched.

The towns constructed for workers in the Ritter Company mills had a doctor, and workers could purchase a form of medical insurance. For $1 a month for a single man, or $1.50 per month for a family, the doctor would make as many calls as necessary. Every morning Dr. J. C. Storie left his home in the village of Proctor and boarded a handcar, pushed by an outbound train of empty railcars. On reaching the logging camp farthest away, the doctor would treat all in need of his services and then coast downhill to the next camp to see patients, until he returned to Proctor, where he would open his office for patients there. Dr. Storie purchased a radio in 1924 and would leave it turned on and the windows of his office open in the evenings so people could come to sit on the porch and listen to the radio.

While the Little River Lumber Company and Ritter Lumber were the largest logging operations in the Smokies, there were others. The Mason Lumber Company sent thousands of cords of softwood each month to the Champion Fiber Company; Norwood Lumber Company felled trees on Forney Creek; Whitting Lumber Company employed four hundred men as loggers and operators of a sawmill and kiln at Judson; and Montvale Lumber Company logged the mouth of Eagle Creek at Fontana. Over 200 miles of railroad went up every watershed and reached the high peaks of the Smoky Mountains.

The coming of the national park, and the felling of most of the old-growth timber, caused the Smoky Mountain version of Paul Bunyan to move on beginning in 1926, and by 1932 he was gone. The Smoky Mountain Paul Bunyan is not a tall tale, but is the tale of people who stood tall. They worked hard and they endured.

Note: The Little River Railroad Museum at Townsend preserves the history of the Little River Railroad and the Little River Lumber Company. The museum is located at what was once the headquarters of the logging operations for the company, and displays original equipment, photos, records, and is staffed by friendly volunteers. There is no admission fee, but donations are welcomed.

CHAPTER 7

Ghost Towns beneath Your Feet

Legendary Lost Villages of the Great Smoky Mountains

Take a walk along one of the trails in the Great Smoky Mountains National Park, especially one that is not too popular. Don't talk to your companions; instead listen to the wind soughing in the trees, the calls of the birds, and the chatter of the red squirrels. You may get the feeling that you are in a land time has forgotten, where humans have left no record of their passing. Then, almost covered with moss and ferns, you glimpse a stretch of a well-constructed stone wall. Nearby you see the remains of the foundation of a house, often stacked rocks forming a rectangle. A path leading to one side takes you to a plot with a few granite markers and many slabs of fieldstone, and you realize you are in a cemetery. There have been people here before you, many people.

What appears to be an untouched piece of nature is actually a ghost town beneath your feet.

The National Park Service has preserved some of the cabins once home to early settlers in the area, but these are not ghost towns—they are well-preserved structures that have been protected and are maintained to tell a story. The Cades Cove area of the park has many such examples. At the Oconoluftee Visitor Center, the Park Service has reconstructed a pioneer farm to show what rural life was like, but this is not a town. Nor do these ghost towns consist of abandoned buildings with collapsing roofs, sagging floors, and broken windows. The ghost towns of the Great Smoky Mountains are faint remains of earlier human habitation that require thought, contemplation, and imagination to visualize the lives that once were lived here.

There are many ghost towns in the Great Smoky Mountains National Park, some of them visible only to trained archaeologists. Scholars in the field say that human beings first arrived in the Smokies about four thousand years ago. We do not know the names of these original inhabitants because they left no written records and they predate the origins of the system of nomenclature now used to identify groups of Native Americans. About one thousand years ago, a people calling themselves the Ain-Yun-Wiya, or the Principal People, migrated to the Great Smoky Mountains, probably coming from the area today known as western New York. Today these people are called the Cherokee. They gave us the first "ghost town" in the Smokies, Kituwah, one of the "mother towns" of the Cherokee.

Kituwah was once a thriving town of several hundred inhabitants who built semipermanent houses and farmed the land along the banks of the Tuckaseegee River. The town was not laid out in streets but consisted of houses loosely grouped around the central feature, a mound with a ceremonial building. Surrounding the town were fields where food crops were grown, with corn, beans, squash, and pumpkins being major crops, all of which could be preserved by drying in the open air. In the center of the town a mound of earth, about twenty feet in height and seventy-two feet in diameter, was topped by a temple or ceremonial house where a fire was kept burning perpetually in recognition of the Creator. Once a year all the fires in the houses in the town were extinguished and relit with flames from the perpetual fire. Kituwah was a center for trade and a gathering place for religious and social events.

Around 1820, Kituwah passed out of the ownership of the Cherokee family and the land was purchased by a white family who owned it for the next 176 years. During that time the mound eroded and the wooded houses of the original inhabitants rotted away and returned to the earth. In 1996 the Eastern Band of the Cherokee purchased just over three hundred acres of Kituwah and declared it a sacred site with great cultural and spiritual significance.

Today, one has to look carefully to spot the remains of the mound, which is only about five feet in height; but with a little imagination, the sights and sounds of the present will be replaced with the quiet but purposely busy activity of the first citizens of Kituwah. One member of the Cherokee says, "It's a very peaceful place. If you go there you can feel the peace. The spirit that was there a long time ago is still there."

Not far from the site of ancient Kituwah are several other, more modern, ghost towns. The town of Hazel Creek has been enshrined in the writings of Horace Kephart, especially the story of how he first came to the Great Smoky Mountains and boarded with the family of Granville Calhoun at Hazel Creek. The construction of Fontana Dam during World War II flooded the site of Hazel Creek, and today its location is under the waters of Fontana Lake.

The discovery of copper ore in the North Carolina mountains caused a short-lived economic boom, during which the town of Adams flourished briefly. The cost of transportation of the ore out of the mountains, as well as legal disputes over who owned the land, caused the incipient town to be abandoned and, when Horace Kephart arrived in the mountains, he lived in an abandoned cabin in Adams.

The arrival of the Ritter Lumber Company in 1902–1903 brought a new town to the Hazel Creek area. A standard-gauge railroad was built up the Hazel Creek watershed to a location where the company wanted to construct sawmills, planing mills, and drying kilns. The company purchased land and built a town with housing for one thousand people, as well as facilities for processing logs into finished lumber used to make parquet flooring. The name of the new town was Proctor. This was a rather attractive town from all descriptions. Facing upstream on Hazel Creek on the left was a row of houses for the lower-paid workers in the various mills, a street humorously called "Calico Street" to emphasize the economic level of those who lived there. These were, however, two- and three-bedroom houses, built of good lumber. All the houses and the fences surrounding their yards were kept in good repair and whitewashed. From the time of construction, each of the workers' houses had running water indoors, and electricity and indoor toilets were added as soon as the facilities to support them could be added. Though the residents of Proctor were in a town and were paid wages, each family had a garden to produce food to help feed the family as well as to save money. When the garden "came in," or began producing, preserving the vegetables not needed for immediate use was of great importance. Green beans were canned, pickled, and dried. Other varieties of beans were shelled and canned, as were tomatoes and corn with the kernels cut off the cob. Cabbage was shredded and packed into large jars, salted, and left to ferment to make sauerkraut. Potatoes, turnips, cabbages, and sweet potatoes were harvested and stored in cellars or in holes dug in the ground and lined with straw and carefully covered with more straw and some protection to keep out the water.

On the right side of Hazel Creek was a row of houses for the skilled workers and supervisors who worked in the mills. They were located on Struttin' Street, an amusing name that emphasized the economic status of those living there. Some of the houses on Struttin' Street were quite elaborate, such as the house occupied by Orson Burlingame, an engineer. His home had fourteen rooms.

To provide for the other needs of the community, Proctor contained a large company-owned commissary, a boardinghouse for unmarried workers, a community center for recreation (which provided billiard tables and movies every Saturday night), a school, a church, and a "clubhouse" for visiting company executives and guests.

The town was a lively place, with many social events taking place during the summer and on holidays. Picnics were a popular social event, and Christmas celebrations involved the entire community. Usually, the residents of Proctor gathered at the Baptist church for a program that included carols and the recitation of poems after which Santa would appear and distribute candy to all the children. The Ritter Lumber Company also gave gifts to children and early teens, and fruit and candy were taken by a special train to logging camps whose residents could not come to the Proctor celebration. Religion provided not only spiritual sustenance but also social occasions, with singing and dinner on the grounds being a favorite warm-weather activity for Sundays. But when the trees had been cut, Ritter Lumber Company moved on and the town of Proctor faded away as rapidly as it had grown.

Today, a visitor to Proctor can take a long hike on Lakeshore Trail, beginning at the end of Lake View Drive, or one can arrange for a boat across Fontana Lake, with a later pickup. By boat, there is a landing at Proctor, at the site where the school once stood. A signboard shows a map of the area and has some basic information about Proctor. Wandering around the trails will lead to the discovery of remains of the railroad that once hauled the lumber to market, the foundations of houses, the crumbling walls of some mill buildings that were constructed of cement and brick, a bridge across Hazel Creek, and a cemetery that served the town and surrounding area. The house that Granville Calhoun occupied when employed as the storekeeper for Ritter Lumber still stands and is used occasionally by Park Service personnel in their duties. Once a year, descendants of the families who lived and worked in and around Proctor gather at the town site for a day of reminiscing, handing on stories to the next generation, and cleaning the brush and weeds from the graves of those who once walked those hills. During the rest of the year, quiet contemplation can reproduce something of an idea of what Proctor once was.

The best known of the Smoky Mountains ghost towns was not a town at all, but a summer resort for people who came from Knoxville and other nearby cities in the days before the establishment of the park. One of the lumber company owners, W. B. Townsend, sold several acres of land from which the valuable timber had been cut to families who wanted vacation homes. Since many of the men in these families belonged to the Elks club, they named their vacation community "Elkmont." Soon a few dozen cottages had been built along the banks of Little River and the adjacent hills, and a clubhouse was constructed as a community gathering place. Officially, the residents formed the Appalachian Club, which had a limited membership. As more people came looking for vacation cottages, a second association called the Wonderland Club was formed, and the Wonderland Park Hotel was built in 1914. Although one of the streets was informally called "Millionaires Row," the houses were actually rustic and rather small.

The remaining structures were "discovered" in 2014 by a writer whose description of Elkmont was carried by *Huffington Post*. Social media made the account a matter of national interest, but most readers thought the structures had just been found, after having been buried and forgotten in the wilderness. In reality, many of the buildings were a century old and their location was well known to the thousands who camped at Elkmont Campground in

Ruins in the Elkmont "ghost town"

COURTESY OF THE LIBRARY OF CONGRESS

the Great Smoky Mountains National Park and to the numerous
hikers who walked the popular trails that led through the area.

As the national park began to be developed, many of the property owners in Elkmont supported the idea, but when the time came to vacate their property an agreement was reached with the National Park Service that gave the owners half the value of their property and a lifetime lease. This agreement did not sit well with many of the longtime residents who had to vacate their farms and homes; they thought it to be special treatment for rich people. As electricity became available in the area, the residents of Elkmont agreed to end their leases in 1952 in exchange for electric lines being run to their cottages. This was done, but as 1952 drew near, the cottage owners renegotiated their deal and were allowed to stay until 1972. The same process was repeated in 1972, but the movement to make more of the Great Smoky Mountains a wilderness park caused the effort to keep the cottages to fail. The final cabin leases expired in 2001. The Wonderland Park Hotel had been closed for years and had become so dilapidated that the Park Service had decided to document the site and then tear down the building, but an unexplained fire in 2016 destroyed the relic.

Because of their age and the quirky architecture of some of the structures, many of the cottages had been placed in the National Register of Historic Places in 1994. With all the lease-holders now out of the picture, the Park Service had to decide how to handle these structures so as to respect their historical nature while emphasizing the natural aspects of the park. In 2009 a decision was reached that, while the buildings were old, they were not truly historic. A few of the buildings would be preserved because of their unique nature. These include a log cabin built by an early settler, Levi Trentham, a "set off house" of the type once occupied by workers in the logging camps, and the Appalachian Club's clubhouse. Scattered along the Jakes Creek and Little River trails are chimneys and stone foundations showing that the summer colony was once much larger. The best known of the Smoky Mountain ghost towns is really a museum community, but it is a reminder of the variety of communities that have found a home in the Great Smoky Mountains.

Hundreds of thousands of visitors annually pass through the Sugarlands Visitor Center just outside Gatlinburg. For the vast majority the stop is a chance to get an introduction to the park, to orient themselves to roads and attractions, and to visit the gift shop. Little do most realize that they have a ghost town under their feet. The early settlers in the area were Richard Reagan and William "Black Bill" Ogle, so called because of the color of his hair and beard; their descendants continued to settle in the same area. Eventually three communities grew up in the Sugarlands valley. Forks-of-the-River and Fighting Creek communities were near the site of the present visitor center, but the larger settlement, worthy of being called a village, was Sugarlands and it was farther south along Newfound Gap Road, near the head of the Husky Gap Trail.

In addition to a cluster of houses, Sugarlands contained two stores selling items that could not be produced locally, such as coffee, salt, tobacco, and popular medicines of the day. Much of the business was done in trade, with the storekeeper accepting eggs, honey, ginseng, and furs, which made their way to Knoxville and the wider world. There were three blacksmith shops and five gristmills to grind corn in or near the village. Churches were present, but the school attended by most children was at Greenbrier until

1912, when Pi Beta Phi established a school in White Oak Flats, now known as Gatlinburg.

There was no good road leading across the mountains to the North Carolina side, only a rough track, which led from the vicinity of Chimney Tops to Road Gap on the main ridge of the Smoky Mountains. This meant Sugarlands was something of a dead end, economically, with little outlet for goods and no prospect for the development of trade. One resident noted, with a touch of ironic humor, "Our air is clean, our meals are lean." The presence of the Little River Lumber Company at Elkmont was welcomed by many since jobs were now available at Elkmont, a location within walking distance. The beginnings of the tourist industry also aided Sugarlands. One store owner, Sam Newman, opened the Sky-u-ka Hotel and installed a gas pump at his store.

Horace Kephart depicted the town of Sugarlands as the center of a booming trade in moonshine, but this account seems to be exaggerated; there was no good way to get goods of any kind to a larger market. Of course, there was something of a rivalry between the Tennessee and North Carolina sides of the Smoky Mountains, dating back to before the Civil War. Each side of the mountains always claimed the other side was a bad place!

With the arrival of the park, Sugarlands and the other communities began to empty themselves of population. A brief respite for the site of Sugarlands came with the establishment of a Civilian Conservation Corps (CCC) near the town site. Several hundred young men lived in the camp while building roads, bridges, retaining walls, cutting trails, and building fire roads in preparation for the establishment of the park.

The beginning of World War II in 1941 brought the end of the CCC, as young men were needed for military service. A short hike along the Old Sugarlands Trail leads to the remains of the CCC Camp and the village of Sugarlands. The trail begins on the grounds of the Sugarlands Visitor Center, and directions are easily available from the staff at the center. All along this trail visitors will have ghost towns under their feet.

One town that did not die and become a ghost is Townsend. Located on the western end of the Tennessee side of the Great Smoky Mountains National Park, Townsend is often called "the quiet side of the Smokies." The town dates to 1903 when the Little River Lumber Company made the location the site of its sawmills, planing mill, and drying kilns. Townsend was linked by a standard-gauge railroad to the main line at Walland and, then, to Knoxville. This rail connection made Townsend the original tourist destination in the Smokies, even while the logging operations were going on. The village was also the main point of access to the summer colony at Elkmont. When the lumber business came to an end, Townsend had an elementary basis on which to build for the new tourist economy.

A visit to Townsend today shows scant remains of the logging activity, except for a small museum, but there are older houses on the old road, just north of the modern route, which give some impression of the glory days of the lumber business. Hikers on the Porters Creek Trail in the Greenbrier section of the park will see many indications of settlement, dating from pioneer days to the founding of the park.

The Greenbrier Cove was heavily settled, with twenty-six families living in the area and sending 225 children to the local school. The Whaley family had a popular hotel at the point where the Middle Prong joins the main river. There were so many Whaleys in the area, often sharing the same first names, that the men were often known by nicknames such as Booger Bill, Whitehead Bill, and Humpy John. The community supported four gristmills, two churches, two stores, and two blacksmith shops. Today, Porters Creek Trail is noted for its wildflower display in the spring.

Walk gently on all the trails. The past is under your feet, and its spirit lingers in the air.

CHAPTER 8

Horace Kephart

The Convoluted Legacy of a Smoky Mountain Legend

One of the most widely read books on the Great Smoky Mountains is *Our Southern Highlanders*, written by Horace Kephart and first published in 1913. More than a century later this book has become a classic with its descriptions of life in the mountains at the beginning of the twentieth century, its depictions of the mountain people, and its chronicles of the quaint, sometimes violent and illegal activities that filled their days. Less widely read, but still popular, is *The Book of Camping and Woodcraft*, first published in 1906, reissued in several subsequent editions by Kephart until it reached nine hundred pages in length, and still read today despite the fact that technology has replaced the gear and materials that Kephart knew with much superior fabrics and equipment. Fans of literature about outdoor living know Horace Kephart as

Horace Kephart on a jaunt into the mountains

one of the most prolific writers of magazine articles about the topic, ranking in popularity and influence in his day with Theodore Roosevelt. People who know the history of the Great Smoky Mountains National Park know that Kephart was a significant figure in the fight to establish a national park in the Smokies to preserve a fragment of the wilderness that once existed in the eastern part of the continent. A mountain in the park is named in his honor and was given his name while he was still living.

This shining legacy has a darker side. Kephart was a dropout from society long before the hippie culture of the 1960s made the term a part of our language. He abandoned his wife and six children to fend for themselves, fled to an area he called "the back of beyond," and had almost no contact with his family after 1904.

When contact with his family did occur, it often became the occasion for a drunken binge. One reason for his flight to the forest was his addiction to alcohol, which expressed itself in binge drinking, often touched off by periods of depression, a problem that haunted him to the day of his death. Although a brilliant writer, he fell into the trap that confronts most authors: writing what the public wants to hear instead of being absolutely faithful to the facts. As a result, Kephart helped perpetuate an image of the mountain people as simpleminded, backward, lazy "hillbillies" who needed outside help in being led into the modern age. His dedication to the creation of a national park would benefit millions for decades to come, but it also meant many families would be forced to uproot themselves from the homes and farms they had occupied for more than a century.

For a person who lived sixty-nine years, including only twenty-seven of them in the Smoky Mountains, Kephart has left a convoluted legacy, but he is certainly one of the legendary figures of the Great Smoky Mountains and of the national park, a man whose legend lives on after him through his writings and the stories still told about him.

Horace Kephart began life in Pennsylvania in 1862, the son of a minister of the United Brethren church. While Horace was a boy, his father moved the family to Iowa. Kephart spent much of his boyhood on the open plains, where he fell in love with the outdoors. The family moved back east when Kephart was in his mid-teens, and he enrolled at Lebanon Valley College, then at Cornell. Following his graduation he worked at Cornell, Boston College, and Yale. Willard Fiske, the librarian at Cornell, took Kephart to Italy for further work and study. In 1887 Kephart married Laura Mack and took a position as head librarian at the St. Louis Mercantile Library, the oldest library in the United States west of the Mississippi River. Over the following years Horace and Laura became the parents of two sons and four daughters. By 1900 Kephart was recognized within his profession as the leading collector and cataloger of material associated with the expansion of the frontier during the period of 1865 to 1890. He was also a recognized authority on early American firearms.

The years from 1900 to 1904 proved to be very difficult for Kephart. His love of the outdoors drove him to take extended camping and hunting trips to the Ozarks while some unknown demon caused him to begin to become a binge drinker. In 1904 he made a move that would change his life and that of the nation: He moved to the southern Appalachian Mountains, first to the vicinity of Asheville, then farther west, and finally to the banks of Hazel Creek in what is now part of the Great Smoky Mountains National Park. Kephart said of this move in *Our Southern Highlanders*:

When I went south into the mountains I was seeking a Back of Beyond. This for more reasons than one. With an inborn taste for the wild and romantic, I yearned for a strange land and a people that had the charm of originality. Again, I had a passion for early American history; and, in Far Appalachia, it seemed that I might realize the past in the present, seeing with my own eyes what life must have been to my pioneer ancestors of a century or two ago. Besides, I wanted to enjoy a free life in the open air, the thrill of the chase, and the man's game of matching my woodcraft against the forces of nature.

When he arrived at Hazel Creek, Kephart had been camping in the mountains for over a month, moving from place to place to find just the surroundings he desired.

Granville Calhoun, a solid citizen of the area and postmaster for his community, recalled Kephart's arrival. Calhoun spoke from memory about an event that had taken place more than fifty years earlier. Calhoun recalled meeting the train, which included both freight and passenger cars, and finding himself facing a very small man who was in poor physical condition. Each man mounted a mule, but Kephart could not keep up the needed pace, so Calhoun tied the reins of Kephart's mule to his saddle horn and got the almost-unconscious man to his house. Calhoun recalled that Kephart could eat nothing until tempted with a small glass of homemade strawberry wine. Over the next three weeks Kephart was slowly nursed back to health with milk, bread and butter, and, finally, solid food. This description is somewhat at odds with what might be expected from a man who had just spent a month camping in the mountains and who arrived with his camping gear. But such a divergence of memory is typical of much of Kephart's life. He had an aura of mystery about him that he did not attempt to dispel, and this has made his legacy convoluted.

After spending some time with the Calhoun family, Kephart sought, and received, permission to move to the site of the unused Adams Copper Mine. There he set up housekeeping in a fourteen-by-fourteen-foot log cabin previously occupied by a blacksmith. He stayed there for three years and found peace in these surroundings; he had only one episode of drinking. One piece of furniture in the old cabin was a typewriter. Almost immediately on arrival Kephart began writing what amounted to a flood of articles for outdoor magazines such as *Sports Afield*, *Field and Stream*, *Forest and Stream*, and *Outing*, making his name well-known to their readers. In 1906 many of these articles were incorporated into a book, *The Book of Camping and Woodcraft*. This publication was a great success and has gone through seven American editions, one British edition, and grew to over nine hundred pages when it was published in two volumes under the title *Camping and Woodcraft*. The book is still in publication, thanks to the clear, forceful style of Kephart's writing. Advances in technology have made the equipment of his day obsolete, so much of the book contains material that is no longer practical, but it remains a joy to read for those who love the outdoors.

In 1908 Kephart moved to Bryson City, North Carolina. Like Thoreau, Kephart found wilderness to be refreshing, but not the place to make one's home. "Home" was the Cooper House, a hotel that is still in business, with an office across the street in a room above a barbershop in a building that still stands. In this office Kephart wrote *Our Southern Highlanders*, first published in 1913 and selling ten thousand copies of the first edition. Kephart revised it for subsequent printings, beginning in 1922. As of 2019 there have been fifty printings of the book, making it the most widely read book about the Smoky Mountains.

Again, the convoluted legacy of Horace Kephart arises. Should this book be seen as a seminal study of the people and folkways of southern Appalachia, or should it be considered a crude stereotype of the mountain people that grossly distorts their life and customs? Scholars have called it both, and some people in and around Bryson City still hold less-than-favorable views of Kephart.

Writing in full spare, like a Smoky Mountain stream after a thunderstorm, Kephart published *Camp Cookery* in 1910. He had earned a deserved reputation as a good camp cook; indeed, it was this skill that secured for him invitations from local hunters to accompany them on their extended jaunts into the high peaks of the Smokies. Kephart was a good shot and could do his share in killing game, but his interest was in the hunters, not the hunting. He would stay in camp, preparing meals for the men who were tramping the woods all day, and would then have his reward by listening to their description of what had transpired during the hunt. Kephart recounted one such scene that took place while he was on a bear hunt along the highest ridge of the Smoky Mountains: "I had made the coffee strong and it was good stuff that I had brought from home. After his first deep draught, Little John exclaimed, 'Ha, boys! That coffee hits whar ye hold it.'" Not all his cooking efforts were as well received. On one occasion Kephart brewed Chinese black tea and passed it around the campfire circle only to have it rejected because "hit tasted yeller."

Does Kephart's writing reveal the man? Does it win adherents for the support of the real history of the Appalachian people? These questions are part of the mystery of this legendary Smoky Mountain writer. Kephart admitted that he did not write about all the inhabitants of the mountains. He was not interested in the professionals and tradesmen who lived in the small towns, nor was his focus on the prosperous farmers who owned good land in the river bottoms. Rather, Kephart deliberately focused on the people who lived up on the steep ridges, where they farmed small plots of land with thin soil and limited fertility. In Kephart's writings, no mountain person speaks standard English or exhibits any degree of education, but instead uses colorful, exotic expressions that depict a lack of formal education, and all of his characters exist in a state of poverty. Yet, Kephart also displayed a fondness for and an admiration of the people about whom he wrote. One scholar of Kephart's work said: "Like the man who wrote it, the book [*Our Southern Highlanders*] is slippery as a speckled trout, problematic as the existence of panthers in his adopted highland homeland. He was an intoxicating wordsmith who was also an oft-intoxicated mythmaker."

As his writings became more widely published, and his audience grew, Kephart kept in contact with people who shared his love for the Smoky Mountains and who were anxious to save remaining areas of virgin timber from being cut for lumber. Some of these people wanted to create a national forest where trees would be cut

Kephart did his writing in an office above this barbershop (window on the left of the second story).

selectively and reforestation would be encouraged. Others wanted to preserve the wild areas just as they were and to protect them by making them part of a national park.

While there was some disagreement about how to preserve the Smoky Mountains, there was agreement that they should be protected. Some members of this diverse group had political connections, others had money, and Kephart had words, which he freely provided as ammunition for the fight. One of the conservation-minded people Kephart met was the photographer George Masa; the two proved to be a powerful team by describing the beauty of the Smoky Mountains in words and pictures, often published together in the same articles.

Kephart despised what mining and logging were doing to the mountains. Once, while on an extended hunt, he was alone on a "stand," a position where game was likely to be seen. The wind was from the north and sound carried for a long distance. "Away down in the rear," he recalled, "I heard the snort of a locomotive, one of those cog-wheeled affairs that are specially built for mountain climbing. With a steam-loader and three camps of a hundred men each, it was despoiling the Tennessee forest. Slowly, but inexorably, a leviathan was crawling into the wilderness and was soon to consume it."

One problem Kephart and other park proponents faced was that logging brought money to many families. There had always been some logging in the mountains as landowners cut and hauled out of the woods selected trees to be sold for lumber in the immediate region. This cutting of a few select trees made a minimum negative impact on the forest. The commercial logging of the late nineteenth and early twentieth centuries, however, devastated the countryside. Still, for many people, the logging jobs, which offered steady work and what was considered reasonable pay, provided the financial security that the traditional pattern of small farming and gathering often could not. But park proponents saw what awaited them once all the trees were gone: an economic crash and a devastated countryside. They proposed another source of income for the local communities: providing outdoor recreation. Many of the park proponents were convinced that, as Margaret Lynn Brown wrote in *The Wild East*, "The East is a land of swarming industrial centers. The millions of people hived in cities have learned that it is a matter of self-preservation for them to have wing room, every now and then, in the open air. They must have vacations out-of-doors." Providing services for these vacationers could be an alternative source of money, but there would be no reason for tourists to come to the Smoky Mountains unless the logging could be stopped. Kephart pled this case in a letter published in the July 19, 1929, *Asheville Times*:

When I first came into the Smokies, the whole region was one of superb forest primeval. I lived for several years in the heart of it. My sylvan studio spread over mountain after mountain, seemingly without end, and it was always clean and fragrant, always vital, growing new shapes of beauty from day to day. The vast trees met overhead like cathedral roofs. I am not a very religious man; but often when standing alone before my Maker in this house not made with hands I bowed my head with reverence and thanked God for His gift of the great forest to one who loved it.

Not long ago, I went to the same place again. It was wrecked, ruined, desecrated, turned into a thousand rubbish heaps, utterly vile and mean. Did anyone ever thank God for a lumberman's slashing?

From the mid-1920s until his death, Kephart devoted more and more of his time and energy to promoting the idea of a park. His books still sold well and he continued to write articles for outdoor magazines, but he cared little for money. Kephart designed a new bullet for rifles that was used by the Remington Arms Company, yet he did not ask the company for cash; he asked for ammunition instead. Kephart's usual appearance was rather disheveled, so when he was asked to go to Washington, DC, to testify before a congressional committee on behalf of the park, a friend purchased a suit and dress shirt for him before the trip.

Kephart was comfortable out in the woods, and he was comfortable in his office writing about the outdoors, but he was not comfortable talking to strangers. He was quite willing to be the writer of material promoting the park, but he did not enjoy appearing before groups to speak on the subject. Yet people needed to be convinced that the park was a good idea. The lumbermen had to be convinced not to continue logging, the US Congress had to be convinced to create a park, the legislatures of North Carolina and Tennessee had to be convinced to support the idea and to make money available, businessmen in Knoxville and Asheville had to be persuaded that they should support a park, and the local people had to be sold on the idea that jobs providing services to tourists were a good idea. The latter argument was especially difficult to make, because it meant that many local people would have to give up their land and homes.

The support of all these groups was absolutely necessary if there was to be a park. Kephart, and the other park supporters, knew there was no definite policy on the part of the US government about acquiring land in the East, but Kephart was convinced that if North Carolina and Tennessee would take enough interest in the park to acquire land themselves and then donate it to the park, then Congress would support the completion of the idea. This is what finally happened. In the western states, national parks were usually formed when public land, which was already owned by the US government, was set aside for parks. The Great Smoky Mountains National Park was a gift to the US government from the people who wanted a park. That is why there is no admission fee to the Great Smoky Mountains National Park.

The final phase of the battle Kephart helped fight was to make the area a park, not a national forest. A national forest is open for many uses, including logging, mining, and hunting; a national park preserves all natural resources from development or exploitation. Kephart felt that if the Smoky Mountain region were turned into a national forest the big trees would be the first to go into the greedy maw of the sawmill. Only by the creation of a park would future generations have the chance to see a real forest, what he called "a real unimproved work of God." For Kephart, and those who shared his views, the choice was between a park and a wasteland. Kephart advocated preservation, not conservation.

The first tract of land for the park was purchased in 1926 from the Little River Lumber Company, a tract that includes the area now called Elkmont. It would be another decade until land acquisition reached the level to allow full park status to be granted to the Smokies, and more years yet until the park was dedicated. Horace Kephart did not live to see the fulfillment of his dream. On April 2, 1931, just a few miles outside Bryson City, North Carolina, an automobile accident took his life. Local lore has it he was returning from a visit to a local moonshiner. The birth pains of the park had begun, ensuring that the dream would become a reality even though Kephart was not there to see it, but when the park was dedicated, one of the tall peaks along the Appalachian Trail bore the name Mount Kephart.

Those who know and love the Great Smoky Mountains National Park know that Horace Kephart is one of the legendary figures of its history; he is also one of its mysteries, and his legacy is convoluted. Conversations with longtime residents of the Bryson City area reveal that controversy continues to shroud the memory of the man—more than one point of view exists concerning his impact on the community and on the Smoky Mountains at large. If you talk with members of hiking clubs or with outdoor enthusiasts, you will find Kephart is remembered as a beloved figure, an icon of the fight to establish the Great Smoky Mountains National Park, and an early champion of environmental preservation. While many people worked to establish the park, no one else has produced a body of writing that has lived so long or that has exerted such influence. One thing is sure: Horace Kephart was—and his writings continue to be—entertaining, exasperating, and educational. It is also certain that the existence of the Great Smoky Mountains National Park is part of his convoluted legacy.

CHAPTER 9

The Legendary "Roamin' Man" of the Smokies: Wiley Oakley

No conversation about the Great Smoky Mountains National Park endures long before the name of the legendary "Roamin' Man" of the Smokies is mentioned. While there are many picturesque characters associated with the area, and while tales are told about a number of them, no legendary character embodies the spirit of the mountains as does Wiley Oakley. Although his fame as a storyteller, hiking guide, and lover of nature took him to many of the largest cities in the nation, his first and abiding love was for the mountains. Wiley himself told the story of his first trip to a "big city," Knoxville, some forty-five miles from his home on the slopes of Mount LeConte near Gatlinburg, Tennessee.

When he was a boy his father asked him if he wanted to go to Knoxville with him to sell the surplus produce of their small farm. Wiley thought the trip would be interesting and a change from his familiar surroundings, so he said "yes." Loading the wagon with honey, potatoes, beans, apples, chestnuts, cabbages, and other

Wiley Oakley in front of the family store in White Oak Flats, now Gatlinburg

produce, the pair set off. The road was little more than a dirt track that crossed numerous creeks and two rivers. Some of the hills were so steep that the pair had to unload part of the cargo from their wagon before the mule could pull the remainder up the hill while Wiley and his father carried the rest themselves. The trip took more than two days. Another two days were spent in Knoxville selling their goods, and then another two days were spent returning home. Father and son camped out each night, cooked all their own food, and acted as salesmen for their goods. Wiley concluded his account of the journey by saying, "I never wanted to go again to the city or market, I liked best to hunt and fish."

It would be difficult to imagine a truer example of a mountain man. Wiley Oakley was born in 1885 on what was then called Mill Creek, which flowed down the slopes of Mount LeConte. The nearest village, White Oak Flats, was little more than a crossroads with a couple of stores, two churches, and a small cluster of houses. Obviously, this could accurately be termed an isolated area. In many ways, life had not changed since the first European settlers arrived in the area: families were largely self-sufficient in matters of food and clothing, they ate what they grew and gathered, and their clothing was made of cloth woven at home from fibers of wool, linen, and cotton. Wiley recalled that several years later, when he got his first gun to use in hunting, it was a flintlock rifle, the same as had been used during the Revolutionary War. It was not until he was older that he got a percussion cap rifle, and that technology had been obsolete since 1870.

The Oakleys were a large family. In his humorous style, Wiley was fond of telling visitors to the Smokies that the family had "eight boys and three girls that we knowed of, but they was so many 'uv us that they might have been another boy in thar sommers."

With eleven children, the Oakley family had to work hard to put enough food on the table.

Wiley was still a child when his mother passed away. He never got over this tragedy, and it became the key factor in forming his character and his love of the mountains. Family members and kindhearted neighbors told Wiley that his mother had gone to heaven, where she wore a white robe and was crowned with stars, a common religious image from that time and place. Wiley took their words literally and began to roam the mountains, climbing the highest peaks to see if he could catch a glimpse of his mother and her robe and crown in the night skies or amid the billowing white clouds that sailed over the mountains.

Sometimes Wiley roamed all the way across the main crest of the Smoky Mountains to the Qualla Boundary, where the Eastern Band of the Cherokee had their home. His mother was part Cherokee, and Wiley found a welcome among her people. From them he learned more nature lore and woodcraft. Later, some people would remark on the fact that Wiley Oakley was very much in the mold of Will Rogers, a man who shared the same Cherokee heritage, since Rogers's ancestors had been part of the Trail of Tears removal of the Cherokee from the Smoky Mountains in the 1830s.

With no mother to guide his development, and with a father distracted by working to support a large family, Wiley had to deal with the trials and temptations of growing up alone. On one occasion an acquaintance said that he had found a secluded place with good access to water and that the location would be the perfect spot to set up a still and make some money. Wiley agreed, with some hesitation, to become a partner in the enterprise. The chosen location was on a small island with a mountain stream on all sides, the land being covered with a thick stand of rhododendron. One day the two were working on constructing their still, with Wiley making part of the cooker pot while his friend hammered on some empty barrels to tighten the staves so they would hold water. Of course, hammering on an empty wooden barrel produces a booming sound that can be heard for a very long distance. Nervously, Wiley warned his friend not to make so much noise lest someone be attracted to their location. But the barrels had to be hammered into shape, so his friend kept on working. Suddenly Wiley noticed a pair of legs working their way through the rhododendron thicket. The foliage was so thick Wiley could not see the upper part of the body. Assuming that he could not be seen either, Wiley went scrambling through the thicket, getting his clothes torn and his skin stabbed with sharp twigs, but he got free of the rhododendron and, with no one in sight, ran for home. He hid in the barn until it was dark and then crept up to the house. He could hear his brothers and sisters wondering why he was not at supper but, to his relief, no one mentioned the sheriff looking for him. At midnight, cold and hungry, Wiley finally went in the house and slipped into bed. By daylight he had decided that he was finished with his one and only involvement in the business of making whiskey.

Life became much less lonely for Wiley on January 19, 1906, when he married Rebecca Ann Ogle, daughter of Noah "Bud" Ogle. The Ogles were neighbors of the Oakleys, with the Ogles living downstream on Mill Creek (called LeConte Creek today).

Wiley and Rebecca Ann made a rather sudden decision to get married and found themselves in the middle of the night searching for someone to perform the ceremony. At last a local minister consented, but he refused to open the door since he was wearing his nightshirt. Wiley shoved the marriage license under the door, the minister signed it and said the appropriate words, and the two were wed by a man they never saw. The two cleared some land on Scratch Britches Mountain and built a cabin there. In time they would have twelve children. Of course, being a great storyteller, Wiley had more than one version of his wedding. A different account is that he and his bride had arranged the time and place for their wedding with a minister they much admired and that he not only performed the wedding at the chosen time but he returned the one dollar Wiley gave him and added another dollar to it as his own wedding gift. One of Wiley's favorite stories was about how he and his new wife settled their first argument when he went off to the cow barn to let his temper settle. After a time his wife called to him and said he was welcome to come back to the house. Wiley concluded that a time and a place for cooling off was something every marriage needed. This story is typical of Wiley's homespun philosophy about successful living.

About the time Wiley and Rebecca Ann were married, changes were beginning to creep into the Smoky Mountains, altering the traditional way of life that had characterized the area for a century and a half. Railroads were being constructed to both the Tennessee and North Carolina sides of what would one day be a national park. The purpose of these railroads was to haul away to urban markets the timber that covered the slopes of the mountains. And someone had to cut this timber, get it off the mountainsides, cut the logs into boards, and load them on the flatcars that would transport them to market. Now there was an alternative to subsistence farming as a way of earning a living—a man could get a job to support his family. The people from outside the mountains who came to survey the timber resources, provide engineering expertise for the railroads, and manage the timber companies saw something else. They saw the great beauty of the mountains and the rich diversity of its plant and animal life, and they talked about these things to their friends and business contacts. Soon a new kind of visitor began to come to the Smoky Mountains: tourists who wanted to experience something of the mountains.

It was at this time that Wiley Oakley proved himself to be worthy of his name, showing just how "wily" he really was. Few people knew the mountains as well as Wiley, since he had been roaming over the hills ever since the death of his mother; few others loved the mountains as much as Wiley; and few others had his skill of spinning an entertaining "tall tale." If people wanted to experience these things and were willing to pay for the chance, Wiley would make himself available to provide what they wanted. Wiley Oakley became one of the first travel and entertainment entrepreneurs of the Great Smoky Mountains. A. H. Huff, another local man, had the money to open the Mountain View Hotel, and Wiley was soon providing guide services to those who wanted to experience the scenery of the Smoky Mountains, view rare flowers and other plants, or hunt or fish. He was paid as much as three dollars a day per person, which provided him and his family with a very respectable level of income for the time and place.

At first these guided trips were made on horseback and by foot, since much of the area had only primitive roads. Once these roads were left behind, a guide was absolutely necessary because there were none of the developed and marked trails that exist today. The dense vegetation and jumbled boulders made it easy to get lost, so Wiley was much in demand among visitors. Because he knew the area so well, Wiley was often called on to help with searches for visitors who had gotten lost. On one occasion two men from Ohio had followed the existing road to the Chimney Tops and had climbed them, but became separated on the way. One of the men finally made his way back to Gatlinburg and asked Mr. Huff at the Mountain View Hotel to raise a search party. Wiley was sent for and the party set off in the darkness. At what is now the Chimney Tops Picnic Area, the group of searchers crossed the river by hopping from rock to rock and made their way on up the valley. They followed the old Indian Road to the place where the two men had left the road to go up the Chimney Tops and, to their disappointment, found a place where the edge of the narrow ridge they were following had broken off. Wiley slid down the ridge and found the lost man alive and well but totally exhausted. Wiley said he was very relieved to be able to walk out of the mountains with a live man instead of having to help carry a dead one.

As his reputation as a guide grew, and his business increased, Wiley moved his family into town and opened a shop selling mountain crafts, souvenirs, and local produce such as honey and homemade jam and jelly. In the evenings Wiley sponsored live music performed by a local string band to draw yet more customers to his establishment. The store also provided a headquarters for his guide service. In developing his career as guide, raconteur, and storekeeper Wiley retained his native dignity—that is, he did not turn himself into a cartoon character who portrayed the exaggerated stereotype of a primitive "hillbilly." Wiley remained himself, sharing his love of the mountains, his respect for their flora and fauna, and his true nature as a son of the mountains who possessed great intelligence and a capacity to learn even though he lacked formal education. However, Wiley was a good businessman who knew what his customers wanted and he provided them with what they sought. He developed his style of storytelling and stored up anecdotes about the history and events associated with the places he showed tourists, and he never lost his sense of humor, always willing to make himself the butt of his own stories and jokes.

Like any good storyteller, Wiley drew on his own experience for the basis of some of his stories, but these were sometimes exaggerated to make a better, more entertaining narrative, and some were pure imagination. Wiley always warned his listeners to pay attention to what he did once a story was finished; he said he never yodeled once he completed a true story.

Scientists, as well as tourists, began to come to the Smoky Mountains as the great diversity of life there became known. Wiley was the guide of choice for these academics because he knew the mountains and their plant and animal life so well, and he knew where to find the unique specimens the scientists sought. One of these scientific visitors was George P. Englehardt, curator in the Department of Natural Science in the Brooklyn Museum. Wiley guided Englehardt on an expedition to collect specimens of salamanders, locally called "spring lizards"; after this outing, Englehardt put Wiley in touch with the American Museum of Natural History. Through these contacts Wiley became quite interested in salamanders, and his native intelligence made him a keen observer of the animals, even though he lacked the formal training to identify them. In the spring of 1928 Wiley mailed to the Museum of Natural History an unusual specimen he had found. Although he was laughed at when he took the jar containing the "quare critter" to the post office, it was only a week until a representative of the museum arrived in Gatlinburg to ask Wiley to show him where the rosy-cheeked salamander had been found so an entire colony could be collected.

With a name already known in academic, sportfishing, and outdoor activity circles, Wiley was an obvious choice to be a spokesman for the movement to found a national park in the Great Smoky Mountains. Wiley was troubled as the timber-cutting operations of the large logging companies laid bare more and more of his beloved mountains. This denuding of the hills not only threatened his livelihood, it violated some of his deepest held convictions, that the mountain wilderness was sacred and should be preserved. When the promoters of the national park idea brought to the area a person of influence, it was not surprising that Wiley was chosen to guide the visitor to special places in the mountains and then to appear at dinners to regale the guests with his stories of "restin' and roamin'" in the hills.

When the park began to take shape, Wiley played another important role. He knew where places of special beauty were located and advised surveyors so that these were included in the park boundaries, and he guided scientists who were cataloging the native flora and fauna. Wiley was more than a storyteller, guide, and entrepreneur, he was an encyclopedia of information about the natural world in what would become the Great Smoky Mountains National Park.

Wiley also became something of a traveler, despite his constant desire to be at his home in the mountains. As both an official and unofficial spokesperson for the development of the national park, Wiley visited New York, Chicago, and Washington, DC, entertaining audiences and pressing the case for preservation of the Smoky Mountains. Of course, these travels led to more stories. On one occasion, Wiley claimed, he took two women on a tour of the mountains and they then kidnapped him, forcing him to travel with them to New York City. In the metropolis Wiley claimed to have been introduced to the executive of a major manufacturer of soap who offered him $10,000 annually—"more money than I ever heared of"—to stay in the city and do a weekly radio program to be sponsored by the soap company. Wiley claimed to have turned down the offer, saying, "They ain't nothin' I want in New York, all I ever wanted was to get back to the Burg." The kernel of truth in this story is that the talks Wiley gave on his visits to big cities were often broadcast; from these talks, he developed a large following, and many of those fans made a trip to Gatlinburg and the Smoky Mountains one of their goals. His following was so large that Wiley was sometimes styled "The Will Rogers of the South." During this period Wiley met John D. Rockefeller, Henry Ford, singer Kate Smith, and President Franklin Roosevelt. He was featured in a newspaper column written by one of the most popular journalists of the day, Ernie Pyle.

It was a proud day for Wiley Oakley when the park was dedicated at a ceremony held at Newfound Gap, where the road from Gatlinburg to Cherokee reaches its highest point. President Roosevelt, the featured speaker, was surrounded by senators, governors, and leading men of business. Standing among them with a quiet dignity was Wiley Oakley, the man who had done so much to preserve the mountains as a place for people to roam for all time.

Wiley did not rest on his fame, but did what any self-respecting entrepreneur would do: he began to promote his services by writing a weekly column for the local newspaper and by becoming the author of two books, later combined into one volume, *Roamin' and Restin' with the Roamin' Man of the Smoky Mountains*.

A life lived in the out of doors is healthy but cannot guarantee immunity to all human ills. In the 1950s Wiley was diagnosed with prostate cancer. On November 18, 1954, Wiley left his beloved mountains. It was his wish that his body remain in the family home following his death until it was time for his body to be moved to the church for his funeral. Following the service Wiley's remains were laid to rest in the White Oak Flats Cemetery, located one block off the main street in Gatlinburg. A simple stone marks his grave. But from his burial site one can see his real memorial: the majestic Great Smoky Mountains.

Many people think Wiley Oakley should be remembered for his knowledge of the Smoky Mountains or for his homespun wit, but a close examination of the concept behind the Great Smoky Mountains National Park shows a greater contribution. Other national parks are mostly known for their scenery and natural beauty, and the focus of the Park Service is to preserve these features. In the Great Smoky Mountains Park, natural beauty shares the spotlight with the unique people who have called the mountains home, and the history and culture of these people are today one of the great attractions of the Great Smoky Mountains. Visitors to the park who view the film shown in the visitor centers are introduced to this history and culture by a section of the film narrated by Lucinda Ogle, the daughter of Wiley Oakley.

CHAPTER 10

The Mysterious Aura of Cades Cove

Cades Cove is one of the crown jewels of Great Smoky Mountains National Park. A visit to the Cove is on the "bucket list" of a majority of those who visit the park every year, and a return trip is made annually by thousands who have viewed the majestic scenery many times before. "Aura" is a distinctive atmosphere or quality that seems to surround and be generated by a person, thing, or place. Cades Cove has an aura, and it is one of mystery.

The only houses one sees are the preserved log cabins and homesteads of pioneer farmers and two churches. Only at the Cable Mill, where there is a small collection of buildings, is the pioneer atmosphere represented. Driving along the Loop Road to make a circuit of the Cove, one can feel a mysterious aura; people have lived here for a long time and the buildings we see are reminders of only a few of them. Why are there no reminders of those who lived in the Cove long after the pioneer period has passed? Why are there no farmhouses to remind the visitor of the many families who lived here well into the twentieth century, when the park was founded? Why are there only woodlands and pastures? Were not the inhabitants of the Cove farmers? One feels the mystery of past residents whose reminders are absent, but the reason for their absence is elusive.

One group of past residents who have left no visible reminders of their presence is the Cherokee. One of these residents gave Cades Cove its name. The major drainage of the Cove is Abrams Creek, named for Old Abrams, the head of the Cherokee town of Chilhowee, which was located some ten or twelve miles west of the Cove. Many residents of Chilhowee spent their summers in the Cove at hunting camps located at each end of the cove. The settlers gave an English name to the wife of Old Abrams, calling her Kate. This name was difficult for the Cherokee to pronounce, so when they called her by this name the settlers heard the word as "Cade." Over time, her name became associated with the Cove, so we know it today as Cades Cove. Other than the name, there is no physical reminder of the Cherokee presence in the Cove, yet one can feel them there. Not all local historians accept this account of how the Cove got its name, so even the name has an enigmatic aura.

John Oliver was the first white settler to establish a permanent home in the Cove, arriving about 1817. Soon he was followed by other families, such as Tipton, Cable, Foute, and Shields; the descendants of these families remained in the Cove until it was included in the national park. Their names are today found on many of the tombstones in the graveyards at the Primitive Baptist Church and Methodist Church. While these early pioneer families made their living by farming, some industry gradually infiltrated the Cove. An iron forge, the Cades Cove Bloomery Forge, operated

COURTESY OF THE LIBRARY OF CONGRESS

The Primitive Baptist Church was a center of religious and social life in Cades Cove.

on Forge Creek, and a woodworking shop was established in the Cove just after 1865. There were at least two legal distilleries making both corn whiskey and fruit brandy, while commerce was represented by several stores and gristmills. The presence of these pioneers is visible because examples of their homes and farm buildings are scattered throughout the Cove.

The mountains surrounding the Cove seem peaceful much of the time, but they can also confront one with a sense of threat, of danger. That was the situation during the Civil War. Who was on top of the mountain, watching to see what you were doing, planning to raid your farm or your herd of cows? Were friends up there, or enemies? The people of the Cove lived with these tensions for four years. Twenty-three young men from the Cove joined the US army, and twelve joined the Confederacy. Just over the crest of the mountains, in Swain County, North Carolina, the people were strongly Confederate. This division of opinion among close neighbors led to numerous incidents of raids, livestock rustling, and harassment of those on the "other side."

No significant military action took place in or near the Cove during the war, but there was a constant threat from guerrillas, called "Bushwhackers." These bands of men were motivated not by political ideology or sectional patriotism but by a desire to take advantage of the tumultuous conditions created by war. Composed of nothing better than robbers, these bands carried out more raids in Blount County, where the Cove is located, than in any other part of Tennessee.

In 1864 the remaining men in the Cove decided to take steps to defend themselves. There were US soldiers in Knoxville and Maryville, but they provided no protection for the Cove. So much food had been taken by the Bushwhackers that many families faced starvation, and the guerrillas had attacked the Primitive Baptist Church, forcing its pastor to flee for his life. Russell Gregory and Peter Cable took the lead in organizing a defense of the Cove.

All residents of the community were expected to play a role in defending themselves, even the children. Girls and boys were sent out on the trails and roads leading into the Cove, ostensibly to fish or pick berries or gather nuts, but actually to watch for strangers. If a group of unknown persons was spotted approaching the Cove, the children would slip into the woods and blow a hunting horn, typically the horn from a cow that had been cleaned out and shaped at the tip into a crude mouthpiece. The blast of sound from such an instrument would echo throughout the Cove and would be repeated by others who heard it. When this signal was heard, cows and horses would be driven to secure hiding places, women would leave their houses to shelter in the woods, and men would grimly take their rifles and disappear into the bushes. Ambushes and confrontations were not uncommon. In one of these skirmishes, Charles Gregory, a raider, confronted his own father, Russell, who was leading the defenders of the Cove.

The end of the war brought a return to the familiar pattern of rural life, though scars remained. The minute book of the Cades Cove Primitive Baptist Church reflects this:

> We, the Primitive Baptist Church in Blount County in Cades Cove, do show to the public why we have not kept up our Church meeting. It was on account of the Rebellion and we was Union people and the Rebels was too strong here in Cades Cove. Our preacher was obliged to leave sometimes, and thank God we once more can meet though it was from August, 1862, until June, 1865 that we did not meet.

Walking through the graveyards at the Primitive Baptist and Methodist Churches in Cades Cove, anyone with a sharp eye will spot tombstones marking the resting places of those who fought on either side. The aura of the past suddenly feels stronger.

Not surprisingly, the people who lived in the Cove developed a suspicion of all strangers during the war years. After the war, that attitude continued and was reinforced by a change in migration patterns. Before the Civil War there was still unclaimed land east of the Mississippi River, and many migrants from the East Coast, as well as immigrants from Europe, moved into the general area of Cades Cove. After the war, people looking for new land went to the plains states, where land was being sold at very low rates by the government of the United States under the terms of the Homestead Act of 1863. Almost no new people moved into Cades Cove, and so the families who had lived there for two generations became a close-knit community.

An atmosphere of isolation and poverty settled on Cades Cove. The economic conditions were common throughout the former Confederate states and affected all who lived there, regardless of race or political opinion. It would be more accurate to say that the people of the Cove were poor in money but self-sufficient in food. The rich lands of the floor of the Cove produced good crops, and the forests produced a bounty of nuts and wild fruit as well as game, so that people lived with a degree of comfort but could not purchase any goods they did not produce except by careful saving of the little money that did come their way.

The families living in the Cove had rather diverse origins; therefore, the way of life that developed there did not represent a remnant of the old Anglo-Saxon culture of Great Britain. Although many families, such as the Shields and Gregory families, did have British roots, the Cabel family was German, originally spelling their name Kobel; the Fout and Freshour families were of French origin; and the Lafabra family was Dutch.

The combination of economic need and personal ingenuity added to the aura of Cades Cove in ways that are still seen and felt.

Fallingwater House, designed by the famous American architect Frank Lloyd Wright, and the Forth Bridge in Scotland are considered outstanding examples of innovation because they utilize cantilever construction. Farmers in Cades Cove built cantilever barns in the years following the Civil War so they could drive their teams and horses under shelter unimpeded by supports on the outside walls. Several of these cantilever barns still stand and are part of the historic landscape of the Cove.

Change began to creep into the Cove as the nineteenth century turned into the twentieth. Logging operations had begun not far away on Little River at Townsend, there were jobs available to any man in the Cove who could take time away from his farm, and new people were becoming more common around the logging towns.

The Cove was difficult to reach because of poor roads, but the people there were not isolated from the changes brought by the passing years. Many of the houses had running water, piped from a nearby spring; others had electric lights, thanks to a Delco battery system; and gasoline engines were being used by some Cove farmers to power threshing machines, increasing the efficiency of separating grain crops from the stalks on which they grew. By 1900 four schools were in operation in the Cove with a total of over two hundred students. One of the larger schools was at the upper end of the Cove near the present-day campground, while another large school was at the lower end near the Cable Mill location. A fierce sports rivalry developed between these two schools until they were consolidated in 1916. The consolidated school was located near the Primitive Baptist Church.

More than any other person John Walter Oliver, great-grandson of the original settler in the Cove, represented the forward-looking spirit that became part of the mindset of the Cove as the twentieth century opened. In 1899 Oliver packed his few clothes and walked thirty miles to enroll at Maryville College, a Presbyterian college founded before the Civil War. He returned to the Cove at the end of his first year and taught school to earn some money, then returned to Maryville for a second year. Deciding that he wanted a different sort of education, he moved to Louisville, Kentucky, and enrolled at Massey Business College. On graduating, he returned to the Cove because he was convinced that a practical application of education could solve most of the everyday problems faced by the people among whom he had grown up.

Back at his ancestral home, Oliver ran a farm of 330 acres, carried mail six days a week on a route that circled the Cove, and served as a minister of the Primitive Baptist Church. The Primitive Baptist Church was once popular in rural areas of the South. Its name is derived from the belief that the original, or "primitive," form of Christianity should be practiced. For example, the church buildings had no musical instruments since such are not mentioned in the New Testament. This insistence on holding on to old ideas about religion did not mean the members of the Primitive Baptist Church, such as John Oliver, rejected new ideas in other areas of life. Religion was its own realm, separate from economics and the operation of a farm.

As a man owning a good farm and with a steady side income, as well as being a member of the oldest family living in the Cove, Oliver was a man of influence. He was a strong supporter of the development of schools in the Cove and set the example by sending his own children to school every day. Oliver sent his daughters to Montreat Junior College in North Carolina, when they had finished the local course of study.

Oliver also kept up his own studies, especially in the field of agriculture and animal husbandry, and then shared his knowledge with his neighbors. Since he delivered the mail six days a week, the term "neighbor" included every family in the Cove.

Oliver frequently ordered new varieties of seeds for garden vegetables. When he harvested his garden, he saved seeds for the next year and shared some with people along his mail route. Oliver ordered chicks of improved breeds, raised a flock, and then shared fertilized eggs throughout the Cove so other families could have hens that laid more eggs. He owned the first purebred Angus Aberdeen bull in the Cove and charged only one dollar to allow "Black Joe" to service cows. Soon the breed of cattle throughout the Cove had improved. The Angus bull was soon followed by a Berkshire boar, whose bloodline soon spread throughout the Cove and brought improved meat production to many families. Additionally, Oliver introduced new varieties of bees and purebred Shropshire sheep to local farmers. After 1910 he was in regular correspondence with the Agricultural Extension Service of the University of Tennessee so he could keep up with the latest developments in farming and share them all around the Cove.

Not content with these activities, Oliver worked to convince families to be inoculated against diseases and then demonstrated that animals could be protected from disease by the same process.

Somehow, he found time to stock Abrams Creek with rainbow trout.

As World War I came to an end, one of the persistent problems facing the people living in Cades Cove began to be solved. The poor roads, which for generations had made the Cove difficult to reach, were being replaced by gravel roads, which were passable in all weather. Now another hue was added to the aura of Cades Cove: tourists began to arrive. Several families, led by John Oliver, built cabins to rent to visitors, while others added rooms to their houses and took in boarders to whom they served meals. Farming was still the primary source of income for most Cove families, and the new roads made the delivery of crops to outside markets a great economic asset. The present-day route into Cades Cove was finished in 1922.

Good roads brought tourists, but tourists brought a dark tint to the aura of Cades Cove because tourism would bring the death of the Cove as a living community. Many people in the Cove were pleased to have paying guests in the summer, and they took advantage of their presence not only by opening cabins and offering meals but by developing attractions for them to see, such as Gregory's Cave, which was equipped with electric lights. Other families offered guides to lead parties to Gregory Bald, Thunderhead, and Spence Field. Talk of a proposed national park was generally welcomed in the Cove because the residents felt they would be near, but not in, the park. This desire to profit from the development of a national park was shared by the leaders of the movement, many of whom openly stated that the establishment of a park would be a boon to the local and regional economy.

However, more and more often the groups visiting the Cove included proponents of the park who remarked that such a beautiful place ought to be included in the park. Such talk aroused suspicions in the minds of some of the Cove residents. Reassurances were offered by Knoxville business leaders and other park proponents that private property would not be taken for the park and that eminent domain was a legal tool that would not be used. It was a shock to many of the Cove families when the Tennessee General Assembly appropriated $1.5 million to purchase lands for the park in April 1927.

Several communities had been included in the proposed footprint for the park, but they lacked the natural beauty of Cades Cove and they had larger populations, which gave them greater political clout. While not the only community remaining in the proposed park boundaries, the Cove was the largest and oldest. Naturally, Cove residents opposed losing their homes, some of which had been in their families for more than a century. A letter-writing campaign was begun, but all correspondence to state and national officials was ignored.

With all other avenues of resistance closed, John Oliver turned to the courts. In 1929 he garnered the support of some of his neighbors and hired an attorney. When the park commission brought suit against Oliver for the eminent domain purchase of his farm, Oliver was ready with a defense. His argument was that the state of Tennessee was using its power to seize property, but the state would not use the property—it would be turned over to the US government. Oliver claimed one sovereign entity could not use its power of eminent domain to benefit another sovereign entity. He also pointed out that Blount County would lose a large part of its tax base since land within the proposed park would not pay taxes. His more emotional point was to emphasize that while families who made their living from the land were being forced to give up their homes, the wealthy residents of Elkmont were being allowed to keep their vacation cottages.

Oliver's arguments carried the day in the local court at Maryville, but an appeal was made to the Supreme Court of Tennessee and that body sided with the park commission. In 1931 a jury was appointed to visit the Oliver farm and determine its value. Oliver appealed this move and again the case found itself before the state Supreme Court where, again, the ruling went against Oliver. He was given $17,000 for his farm. On December 25, 1937, John Oliver moved the last of his goods from the land his family had settled in 1818. Many Cove residents were already gone, and the rest would soon follow.

At first the National Park Service thought the Cove should be allowed to return to its natural state, but it quickly became apparent that this would mean the floor of the Cove would be covered by trees. In the 1940s the Park Service decided to maintain the floor of the Cove as open fields by renting the land so that it could be used for livestock grazing and cutting hay. This approach would further preserve the human history of the Cove by depicting the lifestyle of the period 1825 to 1900. The Cable Mill, house, and associated buildings would be kept to show what a rural crossroads commercial endeavor looked like. The Primitive Baptist and Methodist Churches were allowed to make a special lease agreement that permits maintenance of cemeteries and special services. The rest of the buildings would be removed. The history of an entire era would be removed from the Cove.

Today Cades Cove is peaceful, serene; the mountains are majestic as they rise above the floor of the Cove; the pastures in the Cove speak of contentment and beauty. But one who is sensitive to the whispers of the past will soon understand that the aura of the Cove is a rainbow of both bright and dark hues; the peace and serenity that are first apparent are mixed with struggle, hard work, and displacement of families.

Cades Cove is indeed a mysterious, magical place.

CHAPTER 11

Inspiring Images—Impenetrable Mystery

George Masa, Fabled Photographer
of the Great Smoky Mountains

Imagine hiking through the woods of the Great Smoky Mountains in the 1920s. There is no network of trails, which means a good deal of "bushwhacking" is necessary. Suddenly, coming down the mountain toward you is a very slightly built man, just over five feet in height and weighing about one hundred pounds. He is almost invisible under the mountain of camping gear and camera equipment he has on his back. He is pushing a bicycle wheel mounted to a set of handlebars with an odometer attached, and he is followed by a group of hikers. As the man gets closer, you see that he is Japanese, a real surprise because the population of the mountains is almost 100 percent Anglo-Saxon. The man waves in a friendly fashion and turns to call to his fellow hikers, "More walk, less talk!" As the last of the group passes you ask, "Who is leading your hike?" The answer is "George Masa. You have probably seen his photos of the mountains." And you have seen them. The photos of George Masa have been printed in newspapers, tourist brochures, and publications promoting the formation of a national park in the Great Smoky Mountains.

Today, more than eighty-five years after his death, George Masa's photographs of the Great Smoky Mountains continue to inspire, are still exhibited in art museums, and can be found in prestigious private collections. But while the inspiring images are well known, an impenetrable mystery surrounds George Masa.

When he was born in 1881 (some sources say 1882), his parents named their child Masahara Iizuka. As a young man he studied mining engineering at Meige University in Tokyo and came to the United States around 1906 to continue his studies. The paper trail is meager, but he seems to have studied for a short time at the University of Colorado and, later, at the University of California. Then, for reasons unknown, he ended his studies and spent several years wandering about the country. There was a good deal of prejudice shown toward immigrants from Japan and China on the West Coast. California passed an "Alien Land Law" in 1913 making it difficult for Japanese and Chinese arrivals to purchase land; soon eight other western states adopted similar laws. This inhospitable display may have been part of the reason Masa left the Rocky Mountains and the West Coast. At any rate, a short journal kept by Masa notes that on January 18, 1915, he left San Francisco "on an adventure." He traveled to New Orleans and then joined a group of students touring the eastern United States. When the group reached Asheville, North Carolina, he felt he had found his home.

George Masa, photographer of the Great Smokies

Masa arrived in Asheville in 1915, when tourism was beginning to create jobs in the area and the town was growing rapidly. He
was fascinated with the mountains and decided to make the area his

home. His first job in Asheville was as a cabinetmaker employed by the Vanderbilt family at their Biltmore estate. Later, he worked as a valet at the popular Grove Park Inn and then returned to Biltmore Industries as a woodworker. During his tenure at the Grove Park Inn, Masa had begun to make a little extra money by developing film for the guests staying there.

The Grove Park Inn was built by E. W. Grove, a pharmaceutical entrepreneur who wanted to see Asheville develop as a tourist destination. Grove employed his son-in-law, Fred Seely, to design the building and then set out to create a cosmopolitan atmosphere for the hotel. Masa would perhaps have been seen as an exotic addition to this atmosphere, especially since he maintained a dignified attitude but was respectful toward the wealthy guests who visited Grove Park.

Masa was also a businessman. He observed that guests often wanted their pictures taken on the hotel property, so he offered his services to snap the photos. His sense of placement and composition was so good that soon he was the person the guests asked for when they wanted photographs. Masa also convinced E. W. Grove that pictures of his hotel with happy guests was good advertising, so Grove allowed Masa to set up a darkroom in the basement and to develop the pictures guests made around the grounds and while out on excursions in the mountains. Soon Masa was being asked to photograph weddings and other social events, including the wedding of one of the Vanderbilt family at their Biltmore estate.

By 1916 this activity became profitable enough that Masa was able to open his own photographic business and use his free time to hike in the mountains. At first Masa photographed the mountains immediately around Asheville, including Mount Mitchell. This activity brought good relations with the local Chamber of Commerce that, in turn, brought Masa more business. One of his business associates was L. C. LeCompte, owner of the Asheville Post Card Company. Masa made black-and-white photographs that the Post Card Company retouched and colored before reproducing them en masse for sale. Today, the technique used to color the images makes them appear somewhat garish, but the composition of the scenes and their inherent beauty still make them inspiring.

Over time, Masa began to travel greater distances from Asheville to find new subjects for his photographs. When he found the Great Smoky Mountains, an immediate bond was established. Masa seems to have been touched by the traditional attitude of the legendary ninja warriors of his native land, men who came from humble backgrounds but who still dedicated themselves to living in harmony with nature and to finding personal peace by making long pilgrimages into the mountains. During this time he changed his name to George Masa, perhaps as a concession to the public who found it difficult to pronounce his given name.

With a passion for the beauty and lore of the Great Smoky Mountains, it is no wonder that George Masa met Horace Kephart. The origins of their association are not known, but the two became very good friends and each seemed to have influenced the other. While Kephart was an artist with words, Masa was an artist with a camera. He gave scrupulous attention to detail in composing his photos, showing a special sensitivity to the effects of shadows and light as they played over the mountains. It was not uncommon for Masa to set up his camera and then wait for hours, even more than one day, to get just the combination of light and shadow he wanted; indeed, the attention he gave to cloud formations over the mountains is one of the distinctive features of his work. An acquaintance of Masa's reflected, "George was concerned about and had a sense of aesthetic which is apparent in the framing of his pictures, waiting for the light, for weather effect. He was taken with the outdoors and he had a sensibility about the mountains. He possessed the Japanese aesthetic which led him to be outdoors. He had a questioning mind, searching for trails and trails' details. All this came from his internal being more than an intellectual quest."

Part of the mystery surrounding the life of George Masa is the question of where he learned the technical and artistic elements of photography. As a student of mining engineering, he would have had no training in these aspects, and there is no record of his making a formal or informal study of photography prior to his arrival in Asheville.

Through Kephart's influence, Masa developed a great curiosity about the plants and animals of the mountains and developed considerable expertise as a naturalist. Masa read books recommended by Kephart and developed an interest in the history of the mountains and its settlers, both Native Americans and pioneers. He also began to pay attention to the names given geographical features by the Cherokee and by the pioneer settlers. This store of knowledge would stand him in good stead when the national park came to be developed, because Masa was named to the commission charged with verifying the names of the geographic features the Department of the Interior was considering including in the park. With Masa's involvement, every mountain, valley, and stream within the proposed park boundaries was identified and cataloged. Although some of the names would be changed to honor people associated with the park (including Masa), every visitor to the park benefits from the commission's work as they travel through it.

The relationship between Masa and Kephart also has puzzling aspects. The articles written by Kephart about the beauty of the Great Smoky Mountains were often published accompanied by Masa's photographs. The pictures communicated a message that even the stirring words composed by Kephart could not convey. Yet, Masa did not fit the image of the mountains and the mountain people Kephart was presenting. The Kephart image of the mountains was of an Anglo-Saxon culture that was outside the contemporary lifestyle and progressive concepts of the rest of the nation. In the 1913 and 1922 editions of *Our Southern Highlanders*, Kephart noted, "The mountains proper are free not only from foreigners but from negroes [sic] as well." At this very time Masa and Kephart were close friends and partners in working to establish a national park. Kephart would also say that Masa did his work on behalf of the park "for no compensation. It was out of sheer loyalty to the park idea. He deserves a monument."

The association of these two men was invaluable for the movement to create a park, but it was also invaluable to Masa. In Kephart, Masa found a kindred soul with whom he could enjoy the mountains without having to explain what he perceived to be their spiritual meaning. Kephart became his dearest friend, and his death in an automobile accident in 1931 was a devastating blow for Masa, who said of the news of Kephart's death, "It shocked me to pieces." He made it known that when the time came he wanted to be buried next to Kephart, and gave time and effort during the remainder of his life to keep his friend's memory alive. It was on a memorial hike for Kephart that Masa contracted influenza, the sickness that led to his death in 1933.

By 1931 the movement to establish a park had begun to gather momentum. Masa had sent a book of his photographs to Mrs. Grace Coolidge, the wife of President Calvin Coolidge, and this helped convince the president to authorize the first steps toward creating a national park. A few years later Masa sent a collection of his photographs to John D. Rockefeller, which is said to have played an important part in convincing Rockefeller to donate $5 million to help acquire land for the park. The US government had insisted that the states of North Carolina and Tennessee raise the $10 million needed to purchase the land for the park. A fundraising effort produced about $1 million from the citizens of these states, and the legislatures of each appropriated $2 million. Rockefeller's substantial donation was crucial in the creation of the park.

One of the results associated with the founding of the Great Smoky Mountains National Park was the creation of the Appalachian Trail. The idea of a trail running unbroken the length of the Appalachian Mountain chain was conceived by Myron Avery, who soon gained the support of a number of hiking and outdoor enthusiasts. The trail developed slowly over time, with sections being built in New England, the Shenandoah National Park, and through national forests. George Masa was a leading member of the Carolina Mountain Club, which took over responsibility for developing the North Carolina section of the trail. Here Masa's early training as an engineer came into use, as did his habit of pushing his homemade measuring device with its bicycle wheel when on hikes. Masa personally scouted and helped design the Appalachian Trail from the point where it crosses the North Carolina border with Georgia to the point where it enters Tennessee within the bounds of the park.

The conference that organized the final section of the Appalachian Trail credited Masa with helping determine the route even beyond North Carolina. A leader of the conference, Roy Ozmer, noted that the pictures provided by Masa were a determining factor in deciding the route of the trail.

Other trails bear the imprint of George Masa. One of the most popular hikes for today's visitors is from Newfound Gap along the Appalachian Trail to Charley's Bunion. In 1929 a cloudburst dumped a huge volume of rain on the main crest of the Smokies. Since the area had recently been logged, a hiking party, including Masa, went to investigate the damage. On reaching the point where the ridge fell away in a sheer drop, they found the bedrock of the mountain had been laid bare by the storm. A huge knob of solid rock projected from the ridge, causing one of the party to remark, "That sticks out like Charley's bunion." Masa put the name on his map. Appropriately enough, a hiker visiting Charley's Bunion can see to his southeast Masa Knob.

Another popular trail that has close associations with Masa is the Porter's Creek Trail, an excellent trail for wildflowers in the spring. The original name for this trail was Porter's Gap. Paul Fink, organizer of the Tennessee branch of the Appalachian Trail movement, insisted that Porter's Gap was in the valley through which flows Porter's Creek. Masa insisted that the old maps and the old

This view from Newfound Gap has inspired artists like George Masa and hundreds of thousands of others.

settlers gave the name Porter's Gap to a location on the ridge above the creek. In 1931 Fink wrote Masa to say Masa was right. "You certainly have done a wonderful piece of work in this map-making and you are entitled to much credit for your labors, both in running names down and in the actual map making. I certainly wish we had someone on the Tennessee side as capable and willing as yourself."

Knowing that visitors to the park would want to see what he had seen once the park was opened, Masa compiled his knowledge of terrain and trails into a book that he authored with the help of another photographer and hiker, George McCoy. This guidebook received the stamp of approval of the Great Smoky Mountains National Park, but did not come into print until the year after Masa's death.

Over the years, as more people have come to appreciate the beauty of the Smoky Mountains, there has been a growing appreciation of the art of George Masa. Today he is often called "the Ansel Adams of the Smokies," but it might be more appropriate to call Adams "the George Masa of the West." Adams visited the Smokies once and after releasing only four of his pictures to the public, commented that the Smokies would "be the devil to photograph." What Ansel Adams saw as a challenge, George Masa saw as a life's work.

Masa found the Smokies to be a spiritual place, he felt that if you paid close attention to the natural world you would see something you had not seen before and understand more than you had before. If you missed that opportunity you might never see that thing again. Using infinite patience Masa captured those fleeting moments and has shared them with all who come after him.

George Masa did not live to see the park established, although he did have the satisfaction of knowing it was well on its way. For years he had suffered from tuberculosis, which had weakened his lungs. On June 21, 1933, Masa died after a lengthy stay in an Asheville hospital. The stock market crash of 1929 and the subsequent closing of banks had wiped out all his savings, and Masa was in debt to some of his local supporters who had been providing him with financial assistance.

The local newspaper reported, "With a large white pine forming a canopy and standing as a fitting monument for his grave yesterday George Masa was buried yesterday [sic] in Riverside cemetery while more than one hundred of his friends formed a sorrowing circle around the shrunken form of this little Japanese man of art and mystery."

Before leaving Japan, Masa had been influenced by a Methodist missionary to convert to Christianity, and so his funeral service was conducted by a local Methodist minister. The news article about Masa goes on to state that he was never interested in making money, but that he was an honest and genuine artist who made art for art's own sake. Masa had dreamed of the establishment of a national park in the Smokies and had hoped to have a studio of his own there.

Many of the surviving photographs taken by Masa have been collected in the Pack Memorial Library, the public library of Asheville. It is thought that Masa made about 2,500 photographs of the Smokies but only 1,000 of them have been preserved and cataloged. The Pack Library collection has grown as privately held pictures are donated to the library and as discoveries of previously unknown photos are found. Some of these pictures have been found in family photo albums, scrapbooks, and in one very unlikely place, the archives of a construction company. The company had hired Masa to make a pictorial record of the construction of a building.

Paul Bonesteel produced a documentary film on the life of George Masa in 2003; the showing of this film on North Carolina Public Television made Masa known to a larger audience. The seventy-fifth anniversary of the dedication of the Great Smoky Mountains National Park in 2009 brought another surge of interest in George Masa. The Asheville Art Museum presented an exhibition of his work, emphasizing his contributions to the park. In 1961 the National Park Service honored Masa's contributions to the formation of the Great Smoky Mountains National Park by naming a peak for him. Masa Knob, appropriately, is on the shoulder of Mount Kephart.

There are many unanswered questions about George Masa: why he came to the United States, why he fell so in love with the Smoky Mountains, where he learned his skills as a photographer, and even what happened to most of his pictures. Two things are certain: those who today enjoy the park owe a debt of gratitude to this "man of art and mystery," and those who view his work still feel the inspiration that created them.

CHAPTER 12

The Disappearing Boomtown

All was serene in the gorge of the Little Tennessee River. The water flowed between its banks as it had for eons, passing coves and forests with the mountains standing tall above, the river twisting and turning as it sought its way out of the hills, sometimes presenting itself in serene pools and sometimes furiously dashing over rocks and ledges in a froth of white water. Once there had been more activity along the Little Tennessee. A little commercial mining had gone on as small operations dug copper ore out of the ground, but that had died away. For a time logging had brought limited prosperity to the river valley, and there had been some flourishing villages along its banks, but now the big trees were gone and the loggers were departed. Once again all was peaceful, serene, and timeless in its aspect. Thousands of miles away the roar of aircraft engines over Pearl Harbor was about to change this peaceful spot in the backwoods into a boomtown. Then it, too, would disappear.

The United States entered World War II on December 8, 1941, the day after the Japanese attack on Pearl Harbor. A few days later Congress passed a declaration of war against Germany and Italy as well. Suddenly the nation found itself involved in a conflict that girdled the globe. For two years the war had been going on in Europe, but the United States had managed to remain at peace. Pearl Harbor changed all that. One of the lessons learned during the previous two years was that airpower was going to be an important key to victory. Instead of the wood-and-canvas aircraft used during World War I, planes built of lightweight metal would now be required. Such machines would be able to travel greater distances and carry heavier loads of weapons. The ideal metal out of which to build these air planes was aluminum.

Not many miles to the east of the gorge of the Little Tennessee River, the Aluminum Company of America (Alcoa) had established an aluminum plant in 1910. Alcoa recognized that damming the river gorge would generate the amount of electricity needed to produce aluminum. Thus, three small dams were built on the lower reaches of the Little Tennessee. The Alcoa plant near Maryville, Tennessee, was going to be an important site in the huge increase of production of aluminum needed for the war effort, but another dam was needed.

Alcoa thought their company could build the dam just as they had the others, but the US government was in a hurry.

Since 1899 the US Congress had exercised authority over building dams on navigable streams. The Federal Power Act of 1920 had been passed to coordinate the construction of hydroelectric dams, but did not give exclusive right to build such dams to the federal government. By declaring the Little Tennessee a navigable river, the need to negotiate with Alcoa was avoided, since Congress had the right to authorize dams on such streams. The federal courts ruled that the Little Tennessee was a navigable river and, therefore, under federal jurisdiction; never mind that no boats had ever navigated the part of the river where the dam would be built, this was war and rules were being bent.

Less than a month after the war began, the US Congress authorized the construction of a dam near the tiny village of Fontana, North Carolina. The total population of Fontana was six families, three of them residing in log cabins. The only connection with the outside world was a rough wagon track. The dam was to be the responsibility of the Tennessee Valley Authority (TVA).

Speed was essential because of wartime demands, hordes of workers would be needed, and workers and their families would need places to live, shop, and send their children to school. But none of these facilities existed in backwoods community of Fontana. Recruiting workers would be the least of the problems. The economy of the United States was still negatively affected by the Great Depression, which had begun in 1929, so news that jobs were available was sure to draw the needed workers. Transporting, housing, and feeding them were the real problems.

The Tennessee Valley Authority had some experience in providing the needed facilities. TVA had been constructing dams in isolated spots on the Tennessee River for some years by 1942, and that experience proved invaluable. Not too far away from Fontana was an existing TVA "town," a construction village built for the workers erecting Norris Dam on the Tennessee River. Another village had been constructed near Florence, Alabama, when Wilson Dam was under construction. Arrangements were made to ship prefabricated buildings from these locations. At first, however, the best that could be done was to provide a tent city and a cafeteria. Even the tent city was not large enough, so some workers slept in their cars, in wagons covered with canvas, or in rough shacks they cobbled together out of scraps. One family made their home by hollowing out a fallen rotten tree.

While workmen cleared trees and brush from the construction site and built a passable road toward Bryson City, North Carolina, TVA busied itself with providing housing. Buildings were brought from Norris, Tennessee, and Florence, Alabama, on railcars as soon as tracks were laid. A Caterpillar tractor pushed sections of the buildings into position against each other and carpenters sealed the joints between the sections while roofers joined the roofs. Electricians and plumbers made the necessary connections for power and water, and the building was ready for occupancy. Prefabricated dormitories were provided for unmarried workers. New houses were built on-site using an assembly-line process. One labor crew dug footings for the foundations and waterlines, and masons followed to lay the foundations and build chimneys. Just behind them came a carpenter crew to frame and put siding on the house. As soon as possible, roofers put on a roof, and other workmen did the finishing work on the inside. Painters and a cleanup crew finished off the project in such an efficient fashion that three new houses were built every day. A large facility providing showers and sanitary toilets was built in Bee Cove, an area immediately adjacent to the dormitories for unmarried workers.

As facilities were being built to house workers, another necessary task was under way. The land that would be flooded by the dam was being acquired. The lake created by the dam would flood thirty miles of the gorge of the Little Tennessee River, displacing families and communities from both Swain and Graham Counties in North Carolina. All of these families had seen the displacement of relatives and friends by the creation of the Great Smoky Mountains National Park and they knew resistance was hopeless. At the same time, their sense of loss was tempered by a fierce feeling of patriotism; they knew their nation was at war and they knew the dam was needed to win the conflict. Therefore, there was little protest at having to sell their homes, as their sacrifice was seen as part of the effort being made by the entire nation.

For many of the local people, the dam project meant jobs, some in construction and some providing services. Some of the construction workers lived ten or fifteen miles away from the site, and poor roads and gas rationing meant that not everyone wanted to drive to their job, so those willing to drive took on paying passengers. A car might arrive at the construction site with all inside seats taken, along with even more people standing on the running boards, sitting on the fenders, or perched on the big headlights found on most cars. One enterprising resident of Bryson City covered the bed of his farm truck with canvas, installed benches in the back, and hauled twenty-five workers to the job at each shift change, returning with twenty-five who had just gotten off work. The fare was ten cents per person. Women opened their homes to rent rooms to workers and provide them with meals. A bed, sometimes shared with another person, and three meals a day could be had for five dollars a week. Some of the side jobs were more nefarious. During the summer it was noticed that a truck loaded with watermelons arrived at the camp grocery store every evening about dark. The store did not accept delivery except during the day, so the truck was parked in an isolated corner of the store lot all night. Some of the boys in the village began sneaking up to the truck and making off with a melon. The driver never seemed to notice what they were doing. It was later discovered that the melons covered jars of moonshine whiskey and the truck driver was glad to get rid of the melons.

By June 1942 the population of Fontana had grown from about thirty people living at a rural crossroads to a bustling town of seven thousand residents, the largest town in North Carolina west of Asheville. The community included a barbershop, a beauty shop, a recreation building with adjacent ball fields, a post office, a library, a grocery store, a drugstore, a school with twelve teachers and three hundred pupils, and a jail that would hold three people—people at Fontana were either at work or too tired to get into trouble. A cafeteria was open twenty-four hours a day, seven days a week. In May 1943 the facility served 182,640 meals—just under 6,000 meals a day. In providing this food the kitchens used 21,533 pounds of beef and pork, 10,951 pounds of poultry, 6,800 pounds of fish, 20,190 dozen eggs, 42,800 pounds of potatoes, and other miscellaneous goods for a total of 128 tons of food—all while dealing with wartime rationing of meat, sugar, coffee, and other goods. A visiting newspaper reporter informed his readers that he had eaten lunch at the cafeteria for forty-two cents and that he had his choice of fried chicken, roast beef, cold cuts, a selection of several vegetables, cornbread, pie, and iced tea.

Work on the dam had begun even while the first workers were living in tents. The blueprints called for the construction of a dam

478 feet in height, the tallest east of the Rocky Mountains, and 376 feet wide at its base. It would contain three million cubic yards of concrete. A road twenty-two feet wide would be built across the dam to facilitate bringing materials to both sides of the river. Because of the height of the dam, no water would be allowed to flow over the top, since the force of the impact at the bottom would destroy the dam's foundations. Instead, two tunnels, each thirty-four feet in diameter, would be cut through the rock at one side of the dam. During the construction phase these tunnels would divert the flow of the river to allow work on the massive concrete block. Following completion of the dam, these tunnels would be the spillways carrying excess water several hundred feet beyond the footing of the dam and dumping it against a splash curtain that, during high-water periods, would send a spray of water 150 feet into the air.

By September 1942 both tunnels were completed and the flow of the river had been diverted through them. Work on the dam began in full force. Since the beginning of construction, TVA had used three shifts so that work continued around the clock, seven days a week. Because time was of the essence, all employees, from engineers to construction workers, were encouraged to look for time-saving ways of doing their jobs. One worker came up with an idea that allowed a "bucket" of concrete (twelve cubic yards) to be emptied in a fashion that saved thirteen seconds for each bucket. This idea reduced overall construction time by almost three weeks. Over the next months, 2,171,000 cubic yards of rock and dirt would be excavated, 5,000 tons of steel would be used to reinforce the concrete being poured, and 4,679,900 square feet of forms to mold the concrete would be built.

One reason the work on the dam went so well was that the workers felt a sense of unity and purpose. They were also rewarded and well treated. One of the children whose parents worked on the project recalled that Fontana brought together people from all over the country, people who had previously lived in homogeneous rural communities. The construction site and workers housing introduced them to a diversity of people, an experience that was both entertaining and educational. For many of the families the housing provided was an improvement over the dwellings they left behind. Their new homes were warm, had indoor plumbing and electric stoves, and were well constructed. The knowledge that every worker was engaged in an essential project supporting the war effort created a feeling of unity, even of family.

Racial segregation was an exception to the sense of unity and family at Fontana. Segregation was not a regional phenomenon, but was the policy of the US government. Even the armed forces were strictly segregated by race: the US Navy limited African Americans to certain jobs, and the US Marines did not accept African American recruits at all. So, Fontana was a segregated town with a separate school and recreation facilities for African American families.

The primary material used to construct the dam was concrete. The ingredients in concrete are cement, water, gravel, and sand. The cement was produced at several plants across the region and shipped by rail to the construction site. The river furnished all the water needed to mix the materials, and the surrounding mountains provided the rocks and sand. A rock quarry was established a mile downstream from the construction site, and regular blasts, often three or four a day, ripped away the rock face of the quarry. The rock face had holes drilled into it, which were then packed with an explosive charge. All the charges were connected by electric wires, and, when everyone was clear, the blast was set off. On one occasion 104 tons of explosive were used to blast loose 600,000 tons of rock.

The loose rock was taken by dump truck to a crusher and then was sent by conveyor belt across the river to a secondary crusher where the material was further crushed into small gravel and sand. The sand and gravel were separated and sent to storage piles until they were needed at the mixing plant. These facilities looked like giant farm silos and contained huge machines that stirred together the ingredients to make concrete. At the silo two trains ran on twin tracks across the dam, with each train carrying four to five "buckets" of cement. As the "buckets" on one train were emptied into the forms prepared for them, the second train was loading its "buckets." This meant there was an almost continuous pouring of concrete into the forms waiting for it.

The workers at the forms used both hand tools and machines to make sure the forms were completely filled and no air pockets remained. Pipes were inserted into the forms before the wet concrete was poured so that water could be run through the mass of concrete to cool it while it hardened. This prevented cracking and crumbling. On July 3, 1944, 10,755 cubic yards of concrete were poured in a single day.

One of the legends swirling around the disappearing boomtown is that bodies of workers are buried in the dam, the story being that they fell into wet concrete and sank out of sight, and their bodies were simply left where they rested. History and engineering do not support such legends. First of all, the decomposition of a body would have left an air pocket in the mass of concrete, which would have weakened the entire structure. Second, the concrete was poured into forms that could be removed before the mass hardened. On the few occasions when an accident did claim a life, the form was removed and the body was recovered. Construction records reveal that fourteen people died on the project, not all of them on the site of the dam, and another eleven people were permanently disabled by accidents. This is a rather remarkable safety record.

One of the men killed in an accident at the dam was Bob Carrington. He died when a heavy load being swung into place by a crane hit him. His brother, Wayne, was a soldier in the Pacific Theater and had been captured by the Japanese. When the war ended with the use of the atomic bomb, Wayne was released from a POW camp on the verge of death from starvation and abuse. The death of one brother at Fontana played a role in saving the life of the other.

While production of aluminum at nearby Maryville, Tennessee, had been the original purpose of building the dam, events had added a new mission to the Fontana project. North of the construction site, another project had begun at a town known as Oak Ridge. What was going on at Oak Ridge was a closely kept secret, so much so that the place was often called "the secret city." What was obvious was that large-capacity electric lines were being strung from Fontana to Oak Ridge. Not until after the end of the war was the role of Oak Ridge, and Fontana, in producing the atomic bomb made known to the public.

The tunnels diverting the waters of the Little Tennessee were closed on November 7, 1944, and the reservoir began to fill. Even as

Fontana Dam today

TENNESSEE VALLEY AUTHORITY @ FLICKR

water rose from the bottom, work continued on the top of the dam, with that construction being completed on April 3, 1945. Electric generation had begun in January 1945.

As soon as the work was finished, TVA began dismantling the crushing plants and the mixing silo, the rail tracks and conveyor belts disappeared, and the workmen and their families vacated their homes. In a few months only fifty workers and their families were left on the site to operate the power-generating facilities. The boomtown disappeared as rapidly as it had appeared.

While the boomtown disappeared, the reason for its creation did not. Today Fontana Dam stands 480 feet high and stretches 2,365 feet across the gorge of the Little Tennessee River. During high-water season, visitors standing on the dam can look at water almost lapping at their feet on one side and see a sheer drop of nearly 500 feet on the other side. The three hydroelectric generating units powered by water from the dam can produce 304 megawatts of electricity. The lake created by Fontana Dam provides 238 miles of shoreline and over 10,000 acres of water surface for flood control and for recreation. A road crossing the dam allows visitors to view the facility and provides a crossing of the river for the Appalachian Trail. The road ends at a parking area immediately across the dam. There is a visitor center open from April through October.

Part of the site of the old boomtown has been developed into a resort, Fontana Village, which provides lodging, meals, recreation, and other attractions for visitors. But the casual, relaxing atmosphere present today is nothing like the frenetic activity that marked the location from 1942 until 1944. An ear attuned to the mysteries of the past, and a good imagination, can still take one back to the days when "work or fight" were the only choices for the men and women whose labor produced Fontana Dam and helped win a war. The boomtown is gone, but the contribution its residents made will be forever with us.

CHAPTER 13

The Mysterious Road to Nowhere

It is a lovely drive along Everett Street in Bryson City, North Carolina. As the street leaves the town its name changes to Fontana Road, which leads to the boundary of the Great Smoky Mountains National Park. There the name changes once again to Lakeview Drive; the winding road, with very little traffic, continues for about six miles into the park. A bridge carries the road across Nolands Creek, but suddenly there is a barricade across the paved surface. Ahead looms the mouth of a tunnel, but automobiles cannot enter. If one is daring enough, and has a flashlight, the tunnel is open to foot traffic, but on emerging on the far side, there is no road! Lakeview Drive is a "road to nowhere." Why does this road exist? Why does it end here? Why will it never go any farther? These questions are part of the mystery of the "road to nowhere."

The solution to this mystery is tied up with other Smoky Mountain mysteries and legends, including lost towns, the logging boom, and the rise and fall of Fontana as a boomtown in the wilderness. It also has to do with a long-running argument, only

The road goes into a tunnel and does not come out the other side

recently settled, about what kind of park the Great Smoky Mountains would be.

Before the days of the park, trails, traces, and rough tracks connected several small communities along the north shore of the Little Tennessee River. As time passed, and the economy of the area developed, a modern road was built and was designated North Carolina Route 288. This road was the lifeline for the communities along its route; it brought goods from the wider world to them and took their produce out to a broader market. For those who chose to look for factory jobs, this state route was the highway to work and the road back home when time allowed a visit. At first, the creation of the park did not change this arrangement because the park boundary was well to the north of the banks of the river, and the communities in the area continued much as they had for decades.

September 1, 1939, changed all this, though no one in the area knew it at the time. The beginning of World War II in Europe became the impetus for a great industrial surge in the United States as President Roosevelt proposed that this nation become "the arsenal of democracy." December 7, 1941, made the impetus more necessary and the changes more profound. With the attack on Pearl Harbor, the United States found itself fighting a war in Europe and in the Pacific at the same time. Airpower, the military control of the skies, was a necessary ingredient for victory, and the planes that would provide that control were being built out of aluminum. Thus, Fontana, the "boomtown in the wilderness," emerged. The lake created by Fontana Dam flooded many of the communities along the banks of the river (see "Ghost Towns beneath Your Feet") and covered Route 288, the only viable access to the area. This meant that the communities that were not flooded would have to be abandoned since there was no road connection to the rest of the state or the world. This land would become a part of the Great Smoky Mountains National Park. This situation created the conditions leading to the "road to nowhere."

Taxes! That was the word being spoken very loudly around Bryson City, the county seat of Swain County. Land belonging to the US government is not subject to state and local property taxes; with the creation of a national park, a very large chunk of land in Swain County had just been taken off the tax rolls. The expenses facing the county would not go down, but its income had just decreased dramatically. How could the lost income be recouped?

Family ties were another concern. While the living were being evacuated, the dead would stay behind. Graves that would be covered by the rising lake waters could be moved, but burial sites in the abandoned towns above the high-water mark would stay where they were. With no road, how were family members going to reach these cemeteries to visit graves or to bury relatives who wanted their remains interred in family plots? Family ties run strong and deep in the Appalachian area, and this matter of access to family cemeteries was no idle question. To this day the custom is observed in many communities of holding a Decoration Day on which the extended families of those buried in a cemetery will gather to clean up the grounds, decorate the graves with flowers, and spend time swapping reminiscences of the departed.

Local concern over taxes and access to family graves was so great that an agreement was reached on July 30, 1943, while Fontana Dam was still under construction, to build a road from Bryson City to Deals Gap using a route north of the lake. As a good faith gesture the US government placed $400,000 in a trust fund to help pay for the road. This road would be built through the national park. There were high hopes that this road would provide a gateway into the park and that Bryson City could develop a tourist-based economy to replace the loss of jobs in logging and lumber mills. Those who reflected on the situation calmly saw that the demands of fighting the war and, later, the return to a peacetime economy, would delay the fulfillment of this dream. In 1947 a one-mile section of road was built, which crossed Fontana Dam and ended at the park boundary.

This 1947 construction was all that was done for a long time. However, by the end of the 1950s Bryson City had been linked with Fontana Dam by the construction of North Carolina Route 28 on the south shore of Fontana Lake, and a short road had been built from Bryson City to the Deep Creek area of the national park. Some people felt this construction fulfilled the promise of providing access to the park for both visitors and family members seeking access to burial plots. Also, some money had been made available to replace lost tax revenues.

However, not everyone was satisfied with the idea that Route 28 fulfilled the promise made in 1943. Detractors pointed out that most families still had no access to family cemeteries and that two small access roads to the national park were not enough to make Bryson City a gateway community with a growing tourist economy. At this point the "road to nowhere" became entangled in a larger debate, one that involved public lands nationwide: What kind of park would the Great Smoky Mountains be? Would it be a place that could be viewed and enjoyed from the comfort of an automobile, or would it be a wilderness park, mostly accessible to those who pulled on their boots and hefted a pack onto their back to venture into the woods?

As construction of a road on the north shore of Fontana Lake began in 1960, park superintendent George Fry resurrected an old, controversial plan: the construction of a road along the high crest of the Smoky Mountains, reaching from the Deep Creek area on the North Carolina side to Townsend on the Tennessee side. This idea had first been proposed in 1932, with the road to be called "the Skyway." For those interested in economic development, the road would be a great boon, making Bryson City and Townsend gateway cities like Gatlinburg and Cherokee. One very likely outcome was that thousands of motor-tourists would spend two days making a complete circuit of the Great Smoky Mountains National Park, stopping in the four gateway towns and spending money in each of them. To those interested in solitude and wilderness, Fry's proposal represented disaster.

Wilderness or easy access? That debate had been raging since the days the park was first conceived. Many of the earliest supporters of the park idea were members of the Knoxville Automobile Club, and the impetus for Tennessee and North Carolina to build roads into the mountains was both to provide access to market for local farmers and to allow motor-tourists to access the mountains. The desire to make the mountains accessible to cars led the state of Tennessee to build a road from Gatlinburg to Newfound Gap between 1927 and 1929.

The onset and aftermath of World War II had delayed further discussion of the Skyway project. When it was resurrected by Superintendent George Fry as a part of the "project 66" plan, a new opponent had arisen—a new generation of Americans had become fascinated with the wilderness, and the environmental movement had been born. Knoxville attorney Harvey Broome and his friend Ernie Dickerman joined in leading the fight to S.O.S.: "Save Our Smokies."

Superintendent Fry argued that there was plenty of room for both road development and wilderness. Fry proposed setting up six wilderness areas, keeping most of the land from Newfound Gap east and some areas west of there as wilderness, but he wanted enough non-wilderness areas to allow the construction of the Skyway.

The argument had long been made that the Smoky Mountains were not truly a wilderness area. In 1960 longtime resident Granville Calhoun pointed out that the area had been "picked clean." He argued:

> By the time the virgin stuff was gone they started on the second growth. . . . Man's mark is still upon the land. Anybody with eyesight who travels about Hazel Creek can see the signs of it. Why, there's a dozen graveyards. If it's a wilderness that's never been touched by the hand of man how do they account for them? Or the railroad beds that scar the hillsides? Or the steel bridges built across the creek 50 years ago? And what about the old car wrecks along the creek and the rusting wheels off the railroad cars? That road wouldn't hit a virgin tree anywhere.

The debate between road proponents and wilderness advocates was cut short in 1964 when the US Congress passed the Wilderness Act, which allowed public lands that met specified qualifications to be designated "wilderness areas" and to be exempt from all development, including road construction. Public attention to the environment had been aroused by the publication of the best-selling book by Rachel Carson, *Silent Spring*, in which she vividly depicted a world with no birdsong because a poisoned environment had killed all wildlife. It was soon determined that 475,000 acres of land out of a total of 522,000 acres in the Great Smoky Mountains National Park qualified as wilderness. The Wilderness Act muted the debate between road supporters and wilderness advocates, but it didn't settle it. The Wilderness Act allowed an area to be declared closed to development, but it did not mandate which areas should be closed; therefore, no land in the Smoky Mountains was declared wilderness in 1964.

Although the idea of a transmountain road from Bryson City to Townsend was dead due to opposition by wilderness advocates, the old agreement dealing with North Carolina Route 288 still stood, and slow progress continued on its construction. By 1970 the road had reached its present length, but then the Park Service let the project drop. Six years later over four hundred people attended the first annual Hazel Creek Reunion held at the Deep Creek Picnic Area near Bryson City. One purpose of this event was to pressure the Park Service to complete what was long since called the "road to nowhere" so families could have access to family burial plots. The response by the park superintendent, Boyd Evison, was to ban plastic flowers from being used to decorate graves on park property. This did not sit well with locals. By 1978 the Park Service had changed its approach and was providing boats to help people cross Fontana Lake for a Decoration Day celebration at cemeteries not accessible by road; that practice continues to the present.

Tennessee Senator Jim Sasser had introduced a bill in 1977 that would have declared 475,000 acres of the Great Smoky Mountains National Park as wilderness under the terms of the 1964 Wilderness Act. Sasser's bill was filibustered by North Carolina Senator Jesse Helms. This left the proposed completion of the "road to nowhere" in limbo. Senator Helms attempted to settle the issue in 1987 by introducing a bill to appropriate money for the completion of the road, but this bill died in committee hearings. Following the failure of the Helms bill, Senator Sasser made a fact-finding trip to Swain County, North Carolina, and proposed another bill designating most of the park as wilderness but offering Swain County $9.5 million as a settlement. Senator Helms killed this bill in committee. Clearly, the "road to nowhere" had reached the nation's capital. Throughout the 1990s and into the early 2000s, legislation on one side of the issue or the other was introduced into Congress.

It took a former quarterback from the always-popular University of Tennessee Volunteers to break the impasse. In 2006 Heath Shuler was elected to the House of Representatives for the district that included Swain County. He was a conservative Democrat with deep family ties to the area and was personally familiar with the "road to nowhere," having driven and hiked along it many times. Representative Schuler proposed a cash payment of $52 million to be paid in installments, with the last payment being made in or before 2020. This agreement passed Congress, and an agreement was signed at Bryson City in February 2010. As of this writing, over $39 million has not been paid to Swain County.

Ironically, while the debate over the "road to nowhere" had been going on in North Carolina, a similar, but less fierce, argument had been going on in Tennessee over a "road to nowhere" on the north side of the park. During the time when a second national park in the East was first being discussed (Acadia National Park was the first), there was stiff competition among Virginia, North Carolina, and Tennessee to have a park located partially or entirely in their borders. The Shenandoah and the Great Smoky Mountains parks were authorized at the same time, but development got under way faster in the Shenandoah. A major feature of the Shenandoah

Park was, and is, Skyline Drive, along the crest of the mountains. In the early 1940s President Roosevelt authorized the construction of the Blue Ridge Parkway, linking Skyline Drive with the Great Smoky Mountains National Park. The chosen route would connect with the Smoky Mountains near Cherokee, North Carolina. Political leaders in Tennessee felt they had been slighted, especially since their state had done so much to get the Smoky Mountains park going. As a concession to this feeling, President Roosevelt authorized the construction of the Foothills Parkway to be sited outside the boundaries of the Great Smoky Mountains National Park, for the most part, but giving sweeping views of the mountains rising to the south and east. Since the National Park Service was to acquire land outside Great Smoky Mountains National Park for the construction of the road, environmentalists raised no objections. However, the road would not link any town with the mountains, so no new tourist destinations would be created nor would restaurants, motels, and service stations be permitted along the route of the parkway. At any rate, the road was authorized in 1944, and everyone knew that nothing would happen until the war was over.

Even after World War II ended, progress on the Foothills Parkway was slow and came in spurts. Surveying for a route to bypass the town of Gatlinburg to provide direct access to the Sugarlands Visitor Center was begun in 1951. The completion of this section was the first to open, and today provides a way for visitors coming from Sevierville or Pigeon Forge a route to avoid the traffic in Gatlinburg while having scenic views of that town as well as long-distance looks into the park, especially toward Mount LeConte. For the first part of its route just outside Pigeon Forge, the Foothills Parkway follows the course of the Little Pigeon River, with two lanes of the road on each side of the stream. Just before entering Gatlinburg the road begins to climb up the side of the hills and provides mountain views. This spur intersects the transmountain road, US Route 441, just north of the Sugarlands Visitor Center and rejoins US 441 at the southern edge of Pigeon Forge.

During the decade of the 1960s, construction of the interstate highway system began and Interstate 40 was built around the eastern end of the Great Smoky Mountains National Park, linking Asheville, North Carolina, with Knoxville, Tennessee. A second link in the Foothills Parkway was built at that time. This five-and-one-half mile section begins at Interstate 40 in a gap at the southern end of Stone Mountain and takes the traveler to Cosby, the eastern gateway to the park, and allows easy access along US Route 321 to Gatlinburg. To the south, as one travels west, there are inspiring views of Greenbrier Pinnacle, Mount Guyot, and Mount Cammerer. This is the most often used section of the Foothills Parkway since it links Interstate 40 with the park.

At about the same time the Interstate 40 to Cosby link was being constructed, work was going on at the western end of the proposed Foothills Parkway route. Beginning on US 129 near Lake Chilhowee, this section of the Parkway travels seventeen miles to Townsend, Tennessee. From this part of the road, visitors see the Great Smoky Mountains to the east and south while a look in the other direction shows the sweep of the Tennessee River Valley, with the Cumberland Plateau looming on the western side. At Look Rock there is a trail to a lookout tower. For many years this section of the Parkway led only from Lake Chilhowee to the outskirts of Townsend—truly another "road to nowhere."

Long-range plans were in place to extend the Parkway from Townsend to Wears Valley, just outside Pigeon Forge, but funding and nature provided obstacles. Congress was slow to appropriate money for projects involving national parks during several presidential administrations, and nature offered an additional challenge. Construction of the Interstate 40 to Cosby section had been plagued by landslides as cuts were made through some of the ridges. As construction began on the Townsend to Wears Valley link, engineers on the project reported uncovering pyritic minerals. When these were exposed to rain, they produced sulfuric acid and the runoff into the streams crossed by the project proved deadly to most all aquatic life. Work on the Parkway ceased in 1993 to allow a complete environmental assessment. Work was not resumed until 1999 when an ingenious engineering solution was found.

Instead of using cuts through ridges where pyritic materials were to be found, engineers proposed to construct the Parkway on pillars so that the road "flew" across the mountains rather than ran "through" the mountains. This solution was adopted, money was appropriated in 2009, and in 2018 the Townsend to Wears Valley link was opened. Today it is quite possible to follow a beautiful drive from Wears Valley to Lake Chilhowee, enjoying views of the Great Smoky Mountains never before available from an automobile. There are currently no plans to link Wears Valley with Cosby. The Parkway is still a "road to nowhere," but it serves a positive purpose.

The story of the "mysterious road to nowhere" began in the early days of the park, grew to include two roads, and still has no true ending. Especially in Swain County, North Carolina, there are tender feelings about this topic. But, in a larger sense, the "road to nowhere" did lead to a very important destination: the debate over roads in the Great Smoky Mountains National Park led to the decision that has given us the park we enjoy today.

Note: Although the issue of the "road to nowhere" has led to the Great Smokies being treated as a wilderness area, not a single acre of the park is protected under the Wilderness Act of 1964.

CHAPTER 14

The Story That Would Not Die

This is what the old people told me." That is the traditional opening sentence of stories told by the Cherokee because one purpose of the story is to pass on the knowledge, lore, and history of one generation to another. Recounting what the old people told is an essential part of keeping alive the culture of any people. When the stories die, the culture is gone. The Cherokee have been in the Great Smoky Mountains for a very long time and their story has been told for many generations, but for a time it seemed the story would die because the way of life of the Cherokee was disappearing. The preservation of the Cherokee culture, the fact that their story would not die, is one of the greatest mysteries of the Great Smoky Mountains as well as one of the great stories of courage, perseverance, and survival to be found in the hills.

The challenge to the story of the Cherokee came with their first contact with European settlers. For centuries the Cherokee had used Stone Age technology to survive and make their living. This means the Cherokee had no tools or weapons except those made of wood and stone, because they had no metal. Then the European traders and settlers began to arrive with their modern technology: cooking pots of metal that could be placed directly over a fire, metal axes that could cut down trees much faster than a stone axe and would last longer, sheets of copper from which one could cut triangles to make an effective arrow point so that the precise and slow process of knapping flint was no longer necessary, and muskets that had a greater range and more stopping power than a bow and arrow and allowed hunters to kill larger animals and bring home more meat. When faced with improved technology, the Cherokee did the same thing people all over the world do today: as soon as they could, they adopted the new technology because it made life easier. But with ease comes loss: if all pots are made of metal, the skill of making clay pots will decline and will be lost in as little as a single generation; the same would be true of the traditional skills of making stone axes or projectile points. With the adoption of the new, some of what the old people told began to be lost.

As time passed, the Cherokee had new neighbors: white people who brought their families to live on adjacent lands, much of this land being ceded by the Cherokee in treaties promising peace and trade. Nature being what it is, the young people of each race met and, in some cases, fell in love and married. The children of these marriages were not entirely Cherokee either in culture or in race. New neighbors also brought a new religion, and many of the Cherokee joined the Christian churches that were popular along the frontier.

Sequoyah, a Cherokee living along the Little Tennessee River, just to the west of the Great Smoky Mountains National Park, worked for many years to develop a syllabary so the Cherokee language could be written. When he finished, his method of putting the language into a written form was so simple that a person could learn to read and write in Cherokee in as little as six months. Soon almost all the Cherokee were literate in their own language. While this preserved some of the old stories, the written language also brought news of the outside world, of books and ideas that were new and different.

Then disaster struck. The old friend of the Cherokee, Andrew Jackson, began pressuring the people to move west. Some agreed, some resisted. This resistance was met with the full might of the US government, with the US military forcing almost all the remaining members of the group to move west, following the Trail of Tears. Only a handful remained in the fastness of the mountain coves, their right to remain purchased by T'Sali, who gave his life for his people. Even then, their legal status was uncertain and their title to land was secured only by having the deeds registered by Will Thomas, a man who had not a drop of Cherokee blood but whose heart was with them. Among this scattered remnant the account of "what the old people told" was still recounted, but their voices were growing fainter.

The creation of the Great Smoky Mountains National Park and the construction of Fontana Dam brought some jobs to the Cherokee, but the economic status of the area was still poor.

With the end of World War II in 1945, the Cherokee, like all Americans, faced a changed world. The Depression had been swept away by the jobs created for the war effort, a new energy was driving economic changes that would replace those jobs with new ones, and a new social concept was taking root: leisure time, travel, and vacations. The still-new Great Smoky Mountains National Park would have a role in this new concept, but how were the communities in the vicinity of the park to encourage and benefit from it? On June 27, 1946, a group of eighteen representatives from seven communities and Western North Carolina Teachers College, now known as Western Carolina University, met to discuss this issue. The Cherokee was one of the communities represented. The group adopted for itself the name Western North Carolina Associated Communities (WNCAC). All the members of the group were longtime residents and knew from experience how difficult it was to bring economic development to the area. Two factors seemed significant to many in the group: the presence of the national park and the Blue Ridge Parkway, which was nearing completion. The park would be a draw for visitors, and the Parkway would furnish a link between the Great Smokies and Shenandoah National Parks.

As the WNCAC continued to meet, it was agreed that no one plan would serve the needs of all the communities involved, so separate plans were developed for each of them. The idea that had the greatest appeal for the Cherokee was one that would encourage economic development while also telling the story of the Cherokee people. The Cherokee Historical Association would lead this effort; one objective of the planning group, which included members of the Cherokee Nation, was listening to "what the old people told me." The model the group chose to emulate to tell their story was an outdoor drama, *The Lost Colony*, written by Paul Green, which had been playing successfully since 1937. Green's drama told the story of the Roanoke Colony, the first English attempt at colonization in North America—an attempt that was successfully founded and then simply disappeared. The group decided to have a similar drama created that would tell the story of the Cherokee, keeping alive their stories, and providing jobs for as many local people as possible. Kermit Hunter was chosen to write the script for the drama and was initially paid the rather modest sum of $500. The site chosen for the production was an outdoor amphitheater in the town of Cherokee, North Carolina—a site that was fortunately located so that the sun set behind the audience and the moon rose in front of them.

At first, the people involved in the project thought a drama could be produced by 1947, but this plan proved to be much too optimistic. Work on the site of the outdoor amphitheater was slower than expected, and the writing process produced some conflict between those who wanted a strict recounting of historical facts and those who felt that it was enough to be true to the spirit of the story of the Cherokee without having to document every word of every story. There was even disagreement over the name of the drama, until *Unto These Hills* became the dominant choice. Most of all, money was slow to come in to support the work.

By July 1, 1950, all the pressing problems had been solved, or at least reduced in scope, so that the drama could open. Advertising was sent out, invitations were issued, and the cast and crew made their final preparations. Only one issue remained: the weather. Summer weather produces spectacular thunderstorms in the Great Smoky Mountains as warm air rolls up the slopes of the hills to meet the cool air rolling down from the high peaks. But on July 1, 1950, the clouds did not speak; instead, the words of the old people were clearly heard as every seat in the amphitheater was filled and the sky went dark, revealing the walls of the mountains showing against the western sky.

There was some tension surrounding the drama. Most of the leading roles were filled by white actors, many of them college students, and the Cherokee had only minor parts to fill. The lower-paying jobs such as janitorial work and maintenance work were filled by a number of Cherokee people, but these were clearly not positions of leadership. Good housing was provided for the cast of the drama, while many of the Cherokee people were living in homes without electricity or running water. And most of the decisions about the drama were being made by a group of trustees that did not include Cherokee members.

Over the decades, more leading roles have been filled by Cherokee people as young men and women from the area have pursued careers in acting and in the technical fields that provide support for the production. Today, not only is *Unto These Hills* an economic asset, it is a genuine showcase of Cherokee talent and acting skills.

From that beginning, *Unto These Hills* has never looked back. By the end of the first season, over 107,000 people had attended performances of the drama. At the latest count, over six million people have viewed the drama. *Unto These Hills* has been an important factor in seeing that the story of the Cherokee did not die, and the drama continues to say, "This is what the old people told me."

"The old people" told their story not only in words but also in objects used in daily living, objects that were not only functional but also artistic. Keeping alive the skills used to produce these objects would become part of the effort to preserve Cherokee culture. In 1946 the Qualla Arts and Crafts Mutual was formed with the purposes of preserving traditional Cherokee arts and crafts and of providing the artists and craftspeople with a market where they would receive a fair price for their work. Beginning with fifty-nine members, whose work was juried before the artists were admitted to the mutual, membership has grown to three hundred and is now the largest center for traditional Native American arts and crafts east of the Mississippi River. One of the staff members at the Qualla shop pointed out that many people think they can weave a basket but when confronted with the process beginning with selecting a tree, cutting it down, splitting up the wood, and finding and processing natural native dyes, they develop a new appreciation for the skills of a Cherokee basket weaver.

The Qualla Mutual helps preserve not only traditional arts and crafts, but the materials from which they are made. For example, the mutual has worked with the University of Tennessee to establish a grove of blight-resistant butternut trees to ensure a source of a natural dye.

Even as *Unto These Hills* became a success, it became obvious that more work needed to be done. A realistic picture of the Cherokee was being depicted in the drama, but in the streets and shops of the town a far less truthful story was being told. Along the sidewalks and parking lots of the town of Cherokee, there stood tepees with "chiefs" and "warriors" posing in front of them wearing buckskin clothes and long feather headdresses, dwellings and clothing that fell well short of accurately representing Cherokee culture and history. The image being portrayed was that of the Western Plains tribes; the Cherokee were an Eastern Woodland tribe. The

Cherokee lived in semipermanent dwellings, and depended on growing corn, beans, squash, and pumpkins for most of their food, which was supplemented by hunting small animals with blowguns or bow and arrows. Tourists might be shown what movies and TV prepared them to see, but they were not seeing the truth; this was not what the old people had told.

Even as work was being completed on the *Unto These Hills* project, the WNCAC was planning another project, a living history village that would accurately depict traditional aspects of Cherokee life. The WNCAC's clearly stated goal for the project was:

> To engage in scientific research into early Cherokee Indian History, customs, and modes of living. To study, collect data, publish information, and in every way practicable, to sponsor projects of investigation and education . . . anything calculated to inculcate a wider public understanding and appreciation of the early Cherokee Indian customs and traditions.

Project organizers soon realized that there was very little information about this subject. So many aspects of traditional Cherokee life had been changed or abandoned over a long period that there was no scholarly foundation on which to build a reproduction. Project researchers contacted archaeology departments at the universities of North Carolina, Tennessee, and Georgia for help and began to collect information. The WNCAC decided that the living history village would depict life as lived among the Cherokee in the year 1760, about the time they established permanent

The statue of Sequoyah honors the inventor of the Cherokee syllabary that preserved their language in a written form. Appropriately, the statue is carved from the trunk of a sequoia tree. The Museum of the Cherokee Indian is in the background.

contact with white settlers. The purpose of the living history village was to educate the broader public about Cherokee life, customs, and history, but to do so in an interesting and engaging fashion that would make the experience enjoyable to the visitor.

Careful attention was paid to information gathered from archaeological digs at the sites of Cherokee towns, and traditional crafts and farming methods were investigated as well.

In the summer of 1952, Oconaluftee Village joined *Unto These Hills* by telling modern visitors the Cherokee story of "this is what the old people told me." Stepping through the entrance to Oconaluftee Village mysteriously takes the visitor back in time to the eighteenth century. All the guides and craft demonstrators are Cherokee, and they proudly relate the story of how their predecessors lived and survived for centuries in the Great Smoky Mountains. Men work on constructing a dugout canoe, women weave baskets and make pottery, others demonstrate traditional dances, and, in the Council House, actors show how women played an integral and important role in making decisions that guided the village. Adjacent to the village is a botanical garden of native plants, which tells the story of how the Cherokee used the products of their natural surroundings for medicinal purposes, for dyes, and for food.

Oconaluftee Village has proven to be as popular as *Unto These Hills*, if not more so. By the year 2000 over six million visitors had viewed the living history village. No numbers are available dealing with attendance since that time.

The drama and the living history village were important steps in keeping alive the story of the Cherokee people. They accomplish their educational goal by providing attractive entertainment, but soon another step was taken to provide a sound intellectual and scholarly basis to help preserve what the old people had told.

The creation of the Museum of the Cherokee Indian would be a long and laborious task. A great deal of archaeological excavation was needed in a large number of places, rare printed materials had to be located and acquired, artifacts had to be assembled, and a climate-controlled building constructed to house the material. It was not until 1976 that this work was complete and the building opened to the public.

The purpose of the museum is to preserve and perpetuate the history, culture, and stories of the Cherokee people. This purpose is achieved by a state-of-the-art facility that includes static displays, interactive displays, interactive videos, and walk-through displays showing Cherokee life from various periods of their history.

An educational and research wing of the museum contains four thousand books, thousands of photographs from the 1880s to the present, manuscript materials dating from the 1830s, the William H. Thomas papers, nine hundred reels of microfilm from other archives, original materials printed in the Cherokee syllabary, original materials from the Trail of Tears, and much more that provides a solid intellectual research base for perpetuating the story that will not die.

The story of the Cherokee has not waited for people to come to it; instead, the Eastern Band of the Cherokee is active in reaching out to recount it. Cherokee Friends are tribal members who are experts in their history and culture. The Museum of the Cherokee Indian books engagements with schools and civic organizations, during which these experts tell traditional stories, perform traditional dances, and play the chunkey game—a favorite Cherokee pastime.

Museum of the Cherokee Indian: preserver of the story that would not die

The Warriors of AniKituhwa is a dance troupe that travels the country demonstrating traditional dances and explaining the role of these dances in Cherokee culture. The Warriors were formed in 2003 and have currently appeared before more than 300,000 people. Since 2004 they have made annual appearances at Colonial Williamsburg. One of the Tribal Council members is Marie Junaluska, descendant of one of the most famous Cherokee leaders. She sees the Warriors as an important part of the effort to keep alive an authentic part of Cherokee culture.

Another aspect of the preservation movement that has the Cherokee museum at its center has been the purchase by the Cherokee of sacred and historic sites that had passed out of their possession. These include the site of the Kituwah Mound, once surrounded by the "mother town," and the nearby Cowee Mound and Tallulah Mound. The home of Sequoyah, where the syllabary was developed, is preserved by the state of Tennessee.

If a story is to be told accurately and if it is to keep a life of its own, the story must have a language. Currently there are about 15,000 members of the Eastern Band of the Cherokee Nation but only about 180 are fluent in the Cherokee language. One reason for the small number of people fluent in the language is that for many years all Cherokee children were forced to attend schools where the language was not spoken; indeed, its use was discouraged if not forbidden. Fortunately, some older family members continued to speak Cherokee at home and passed on the language to their children and grandchildren.

Today, policies and attitudes about the Cherokee language have changed. Students learn the basics of the language in public schools, and the state of North Carolina has agreed that those who teach the language do not have to be qualified in other areas to teach Cherokee in the public schools. There is an immersion program in which both children and adults meet for language lessons outside the formal school system and speak only Cherokee for an entire day. And even street signs in the town of Cherokee are now written in Cherokee as well as English, reminding everyone that the Cherokee have their own culture and their own language. Saving a language is not an easy task, and it is possible that the Cherokee may yet lose their language, but strong efforts are being made to see that what the old people told is retold in the original tongue.

For a time it appeared that outside cultural forces would destroy the Cherokee way of life, but while the flames sometimes died away to only glowing embers, the story would not die. Pride in their past, a value placed on their history, and a recognition of the positive elements of their culture have kept the story of the Cherokee alive.

"This is what the old people told me" is a story still being told.

BIBLIOGRAPHY

Banker, Mark. *Appalachians All: East Tennesseans and the Elusive History of an American Region*. Knoxville: University of Tennessee Press, 2010.

"Black Jack Davy," The Max Hunter Folk Song Collection, accessed November 12, 2018, https://maxhunter.missouristate.edu/songinformation.aspx?ID=831.

Brewer, Alberta, and Carson Brewer. *Valley So Wild: A Folk History*. Knoxville: East Tennessee Historical Society, 1975.

Brown, Margaret Lynn. *The Wild East: A Biography of the Great Smoky Mountains* Tallahassee. University Press of Florida, 2000.

Bush, Florence Cope. *Dorie: Woman of the Mountains*. Knoxville: University of Tennessee Press, 1992.

Casada, Jim. "George Masa." *North Carolina Encyclopedia*. Raleigh: University of North Carolina Press, 2006.

———. "The Most Popular Outdoor Writer." *Sporting Classics*, November/December, 2014.

"Charles Enloe Moore," January 12, 2012, www.charlesmoore archaeology.com/about-charles.

Connor, Jr., William P. *History of Cherokee Historical Association: 1946–1982*. Cherokee, NC: Cherokee Historical Association, 1982.

Crozier, Ethelred W. *White-Caps: A History of the Organization in Sevier County*. Knoxville: Bean, Warters & Gault, Printers & Binders, 1899. Reprint by Forgotten Books: London, 2018.

Cummings, William Joseph. "Community, Violence, and the Nature of Change: Whitecapping in Sevier County, Tennessee, During the 1890's." Master's Thesis. Knoxville: University of Tennessee, 1988. TRACE: Tennessee Research and Creative Exchange, https://trace .tennessee.edu/utk_gradthes/8.

De Bruhl, Marshall. *Sword of San Jacinto: A Life of Sam Houston.* New York: Random House, 1993.

"Discover Kituwah Mound, Cherokee Mother Town, at Two Upcoming Run/Walk Events," April 18, 2017, http://visitcherokeenc.com/ blog/entry/discover-kituwah-mound-cherokee-mother-town-at-two -upcoming-run-walk-events.

Donald, David H. *Lincoln.* New York: Simon & Schuster, 1995.

Dunn, Durwood. *Cades Cove: The Life and Death of a Southern Appalachian Community.* Knoxville: University of Tennessee Press, 1988.

Elliot, Ruth G. "The Fontana Story," GranhamCounty.net, accessed September 9, 2019, www.grahamcounty.net/GCHistory/08-fontana/ fontana.htm.

Enloe, R. Vincent. *The Abraham Lincoln Cover-up.* New Providence, NJ: Genealogy Today Publications, 2001.

Fishman, Jason. "The Incredible True Story of Wiley Oakley: The Roamin' Man of the Mountains." *Visit My Smokies,* June 25, 2018, www.visitmysmokies.com/blog/smoky-mountains/the-story-of-wiley -oakley.

Frome, Michael. *Strangers in High Places: The Story of the Great Smoky Mountains.* Garden City, NY: Doubleday & Company, 1966.

"George Masa's Funeral Is Held at Church Here," *Citizen Times* (Asheville), June 24, 1933.

"Gravesite of Nancy Hanks Lincoln," National Park Service, accessed March 7, 2019, www.nps.gov/places/grave-site-of-nancy-hanks -lincoln.htm.

Great Smoky Mountains Colloquy, 13, no. 1 (Spring 2012). Knoxville: University of Tennessee Press.

Gregory, Jack, and Rennard Strickland. *Sam Houston With the Cherokees: 1829–1833*. Norman: University of Oklahoma Press, 1967.

Guttman, Amy. "Criminal Lawyer Cashes in on Moonshine," *Forbes*, December 23, 2014.

Haer Manuscript, unpublished. "Roads and Bridges of the Great Smoky Mountains National Park. McClung Library Special Collections, University of Tennessee, Knoxville.

Hardy, Michael C. *Kirk's Civil War Raids Along the Blue Ridge*. Charleston, SC: The History Press, 2018.

Hart, Bill. "George Masa: The Best Mountaineer." *May We All Remember Well*, Vol. 1. Edited by Robert S. Brunk. Asheville: Robert S. Brunk Auction Services, 1997.

———. "Photographer George Masa." *Smokies Life*, 2, no. 2, 76–85.

Holland, Lance. *Fontana: A Pocket History of Appalachia*. Robbinsville, NC: Appalachian History, 2001.

"Horace Kephart and the Smoky Mountains," Piddlin.com, July 21, 2017, https://piddlin.com/library/smoky-mountains/horace -kephart.

"Houston, Samuel," *The Handbook of Texas Online*, accessed September 18, 2018, www.tsha.utexas.edu/handbook/online/ articles/view/HH/fho73.html.

Ignatova, Kat. "George Masa," November 2, 2015, www.thetrek.com/ park-history-profile-georgemasa.

"Israel Alexander Hatcher," Tripod, accessed December 7, 2018, http:// huskey-ogle-family.tripod.com/ancestorarchives/id16.html.

Johnson, Becky. "A Call to Service." *Smoky Mountain Living*, August 1, 2013.

Joyner, Charles. "Was Abraham Lincoln Born in Western North Carolina?" *Carolina Country*, February 2003.

Kephart, Horace. *Our Southern Highlanders: A Narrative of Adventure in the Southern Appalachians and a Study of Life Among the Mountaineers.* Knoxville: The University of Tennessee Press, 1976. First edition, 1913. Revised edition, 1922.

Marsico, Christi. "Nancy Dude: Legend, Murderer, Victim." *Smoky Mountain News*, December 10, 2008.

"Marvin 'Popcorn' Sutton," Find a Grave, accesses October 27, 2018, www.findagrave.com/memorial/183886429/marvin-sutton.

McCade, Arthur "Butch." "Wiley Oakley: Roamin' Man of the Mountains." *The Mountain News,* April 7, 2013.

McMahan, Carroll. "Man of the Mountains." *Smoky Mountain Living*, August 1, 2014, www.smliv.com/stories/man-of-the-mountains.

McMahan, Carroll. "Upland Chronicles: Sheriff Maples Takes on White Caps," accessed December 3, 2018, http://mountainpress.uber .matchbin.net/printer_friendly/9038804.

"Museum Archives," Museum of the Cherokee Indian, accessed August 1, 2018, www.cherokeemuseum.org/archives.

Neufeld, Rob. "George Masa, photographer and Great Smoky Mountain explorer," May 6, 2013. www.thereadonwnc.ning.com, May 6, 2013.

Oakley, Wiley. *Roamin' & Restin' With the Roamin' Man of the Smoky Mountains.* Gatlinburg, TN: Oakley Books, 1986. Originally published 1940.

"Our History," Tennessee Valley Authority, accessed September 14, 2018, www.tva.gov/About-TVA/Our-History.

Paludan, Philip S. *Victims: A True Story of the Civil War.* Knoxville: The University of Tennessee Press, 1981.

•

Pierce, Daniel S. *Corn from a Jar: Moonshining in the Great Smoky Mountains*. Knoxville: Great Smoky Mountains Association, 2013.

———. *Hazel Creek: The Life and Death of an Iconic Mountain Community*. Gatlinburg, TN: Great Smoky Mountains Association, 2017.

———. "Timber! Ritter Lumber Company Comes to Hazel Creek." *Smokies Life*, 11, no. 1, 28–39.

Pinkerton, J. C. "Cherokee Wife of Sam Houston," Paradise Text History, accessed September 18, 2018, https://sites.google.com/site/paradisetexashistory/articles/cherokee-wife-of-sam-houston.

Race, Paul D. "History of the Little River Railroad and Lumber Company," Family Garden Trains, accessed February 4, 2019, https://familygardentrains.com/primer/prototype/little_river/little_river_history.htm.

"The Republic of Texas and the Cherokee Indians," Native American Net Roots, March 25, 2010, http://nativeamericannetroots.net/diary/429.

"Sam Houston, The Man," Historic Sam Houston Schoolhouse, accessed January 9, 2019, http://samhoustonhistoricschoolhouse.org/sam-houston-the-man.

Shields, A. Randolph. *The Cades Cove Story*. Gatlinburg, TN: Great Smoky Mountains Natural History Association, 1977.

Stanley, Maurice. *The Legend of Nancy Dude*. Winston-Salem, NC: John F. Blair, Publisher, 1991. (Note from author: Although this book is fiction, it is based on careful research and contains an appendix of factual material.)

———. "Nancy Dude: Boogeywoman of the Smokies. *Smokies Life*, 7, no. 2, 22–31.

Steers, Edward Jr. "Abraham Lincoln's Paternity," accessed July 16, 2018, www.abrahamlincolnonline.org/lincoln/education/father.htm.

Stewart, Bruce E. *King of the Moonshiners: Lewis R. Redmond in Fact & Fiction*. Knoxville: The University of Tennessee Press, 2008.

Talbot, Frederick A. "The Shay Geared Locomotive," Railway Wonders of the World, accessed February 19, 2019, www.railway wondersoftheworld.com/shay-locomotive.html.

Turpin, James A. *The Serpent Slips into a Modern Eden*. Raleigh, NC: Edwards and Broughton, 1923. Second edition, 1993.

WBIR. "Wiley Oakley's 'The Cow Barn,' The Heartland Series, February 12, 2018, WBIRHeartlandSeries/videos/wiley-oakleys-the -cow-barn/10157170960760550.

Weals, Vic. *Last Train to Elkmont: A Look Back at Life on Little River in the Great Smoky Mountains*. Kodak, TN: Olden Press, 1993.

"White Caps and Blue Bills of the Smoky Mountains and East Tennessee," Pioneer Vacation Rentals, accessed December 3, 2018, https://pioneerrents.com/information-center/white-caps-and-blue -bills.

Williams, Don. "Night Riders from Hell: White Caps in Sevier County," *Smokies Life*, 11, no. 1, 18–27.

Zines, L. S. "The Invisible George Masa," *Medium*, May 21, 2018, https://medium.com/@LSzines/the-invisible-george-masa -10bdd4759c91.

INDEX

A

Abrams Creek, 119, 127
Adams, Ansel, 141
Adams Copper Mine, 96
Adams, Tennessee, 81
Ain-Yun-Wiya, 79
Alien Land Law, 132
Allen, Eliza, 8, 10
aluminum, 145, 153, 158
Aluminum Company of America
  (Alcoa), 145
American Museum of Natural
  History, 113
Appalachian Club, 84
Appalachian Trail, 104, 138, 139, 155
Arkansas Gazette, 10
Arthur, Chester A., 55
Asheville Art Museum, 143
Asheville, North Carolina, 102, 132,
  133, 135, 136, 142, 149, 166
Asheville Post Card Company, 135
Asheville Times, 101
Ashe, William, 67
atomic bomb production, 153
Avery, Myron, 138
Ayers, Horace, 67

B

Babe the Blue Ox, 65
Baker, Joe, 63, 64
Baldwin engines, 72
Barton, William E., 24
Battle of the Alamo, 12
Bee Cove, 147
Black, S. A., 49
blockading, 54
Blue Bills, 32, 33
Blue Ridge Parkway, 165, 172
Bonesteel, Paul, 143
Book of Camping and Woodcraft, The,
  91, 96
Bowl (Cherokee leader), 12, 13
Breeden, Bell, 32
Breeden, Jess, 32
Breeden, Martha, 32
Breeden, Mary, 32
Brooklyn Museum, 113
Broome, Harvey, 161
Brown, Margaret Lynn, 101
Bryson City, North Carolina, 41, 49,
  50, 52, 54, 57, 96, 104, 147, 148,
  156, 158, 159, 160, 163, 164
Buckner, Louis, 25
Bunyan, Paul, 65

Burlingame, Orson, 82
Bushwhackers, 121

C
Cable Mill, 118
Cable, Peter, 121
Cades Cove, 57, 79, 118, 119, 120, 121, 122, 123, 124, 125, 126, 127, 128, 129, 130
Cades Cove Bloomery Forge, 119
Calhoun, Granville, 81, 83, 95, 162
Calhoun, John C., 11
Camp Cookery, 97
cantilever barns, 124
Carden, Gary, 50
Carolina Mountain Club, 138
Carrington, Bob, 153
Carrington, Wayne, 153
Carson, Rachel, 162
Carver, Jack, 47, 48
Caswell, James, 24
Cathey, James H., 23
Catlett, J. W., 34, 35, 37
Chandler, Lizzie, 35
Charley's Bunion, 139
Cherokee, 2, 5, 7, 8, 9, 10, 12, 52, 79, 80, 108, 119, 136, 169, 170, 171, 173, 174, 175, 178, 179, 181, 182
Cherokee Friends, 179
Cherokee Historical Association, 172
Cherokee language, 171, 181
Cherokee Nation, 1, 6, 10, 12, 172, 181
Cherokee, North Carolina, 116, 160, 165, 173, 181

Cherokee, preserving culture, 169, 173, 174, 175, 177, 178, 179, 180, 182
Chicago Tribune, 17
Chilhowee, 119
Chimney Tops, 112
Civilian Conservation Corps (CCC), 88, 89
Civil War, 22, 34, 36, 41, 42, 51, 52, 88, 120
Clay, Henry, 8
Coburn, Jack, 66
Coffee County, Tennessee, 63
Coloneh, "the raven", 4
Conard, John, 41, 42, 43
Conard, Kathleen, 41, 43
concrete, making of, 151
Coolidge, Calvin, 138
Coolidge, Grace, 138
Cooper, Elias, 57
Cooper House, 96
Cope, Dorie, 75
Cosby, Tennessee, 59, 166, 167
Costner, Ike, 59
county poor farm, 46
Cowee Mound, 181
Creek Indians, 5
Crittenden, Edward B., 56

D
dams, 145, 146, 148, 149, 150, 151, 153, 154
Davis, Thomas, 33, 35, 37, 38
Decoration Day, 159, 163
Denton, Dick, 59
Dickerman, Ernie, 161

doogaloo, 74

dry states, 58

Dude, Nancy, 40, 41, 42, 43, 44, 45, 46, 47, 48, 49, 50

Due, Jennie, 4

E

economic concerns, 100

economics, making whiskey, 62

Edgerton, Dr., 17

Elkmont, 84, 86, 88, 89, 103, 129

Elkmont Campground, 73

eminent domain, 128

Englehardt, George P., 113

Enloe, Abraham, 14, 16, 20, 21, 22, 26

Enloe, Abraham, Jr., 16, 22, 26

Enloe, Abraham, Mrs., 16, 17

Enloe, Wesley, 22, 23

environmental concerns, 70, 71, 161, 167

environmental conservation, 103

environmental preservation, 103, 104, 114, 115

Erwin, John P., 8

Esquire, 59

Evison, Boyd, 163

excise tax, whiskey, 52

F

Fallingwater House, 124

family graves, access, 159, 160, 163

Federal Power Act of 1920, 145

Ferguson, Garland S., 48

Field and Stream, 96

Fincher, W. T., 47

Fink, Paul, 139

Fisher, John W., 68

Fiske, Willard, 94

Fontana Dam, 81, 154, 155, 158, 159, 171

Fontana Lake, 81, 83, 160, 163

Fontana, North Carolina, 146, 149, 151, 153, 156, 158

Fontana Village, 155

Foothills Parkway, 165, 166

Ford, Henry, 115

Forest and Stream, 96

Forth Bridge (Scotland), 124

Fort Williams, 6

Fry, George, 160, 161

G

Gallaher, Austin, 18

Garrett, George, 44

Gatlinburg, Tennessee, 64, 87, 88, 105, 112, 114, 115, 116, 160, 161, 165, 166

ghost towns, 79, 84, 87

Goodnight, Jerry, 26

granny woman, 40

Great Depression, 146

Great Smoky Mountains National Park, 2, 16, 19, 25, 26, 27, 28, 50, 57, 59, 65, 73, 78, 79, 85, 89, 92, 103, 104, 105, 115, 116, 118, 138, 141, 143, 148, 156, 158, 161, 162, 163, 166, 168, 170, 171, 172

Green, Paul, 172

Greenbrier Pinnacle, 166

Gregory, Charles, 122

Gregory, Josiah, 58

Gregory, Russell, 121, 122
Grove, E. W., 134
Grove Park Inn, 134
Gunter, Robert, 59

H
Hanks, Lucy, 17
Hannah, Dude, 43, 44, 48
Hatcher, Israel Alexander, 36, 38
Hazel Creek, 66, 67, 68, 73, 81, 82,
    83, 95
Hazel Creek Reunion, 163
Head, Reverend Jesse, 18
Helms, Jesse, 163
Helton, Elijah, 33
Henderson, J. A., 32
Henderson Springs, 33
Hermitage, The, 8
Herndon, William H., 17, 21
Hicks, W. R., 29
Higdon, 75, 76
Hillbilly: The Real Story, 60
Homestead Act of 1863, 123
Horseshoe Bend, battle, 5, 8, 9
Houston, Sam, 1, 3, 4, 5, 6, 7, 8, 9, 10,
    11, 12, 13
Houston, Sam, duel, 8
Houston, Sam, governor of
    Tennessee, 8
Houston, Sam, President of the
    Republic of Texas, 13
Houston, Sam, US House of
    Representatives, 8, 11
Huff, A. H., 111, 112
Huffington Post, 84
Hunter, Kermit, 173

Hutchison, Neal, 60

I
immigration, 31
indentured servant, 15
independent tribal nation, 7

J
Jackson, Andrew, 5, 6, 7, 8, 171
James, Frank, 48
Johnson, Junior, 59
Johnson, Robert Glenn, Sr., 59
Junaluska, Marie, 180

K
Kephart, Horace, 58, 62, 81, 88, 91,
    93, 94, 95, 96, 97, 98, 100, 102,
    103, 104, 135, 136, 137
Kephart, Horace, death, 104, 137
Kerley, Howard, 42, 44, 49
Kerley, Nancy (aka Nancy Dude), 40
Kerley, William Henry, 42, 43, 44,
    49, 50
Key, Francis Scott, 11
Kirk, Robert, 42
Kituwah, 79, 80, 81
Kituwah Mound, 180
Knoxville Automobile Club, 161
Knoxville, Tennessee, 31, 63, 66, 68,
    84, 87, 89, 102, 105, 121, 166

L
Lake Chilhowee, 166
Lakeview Drive, 156
Lamon, Ward, 21
Last One, The, 60

Lea, Margaret Moffette, 11
LeCompte, L. C., 135
LeConte Creek, 109
Legend of Nancy Dude, The, 50
Lima Locomotive Works, 72
Lincoln, Abraham, 14, 16, 17, 18, 19, 21, 22, 24, 26
Lincoln Center, 26
Lincoln County, Tennessee, 63
Lincoln Festival, 26
Lincoln Hill, 26
Lincoln Memorial, 24
Lincoln, Nancy Hanks, 15, 16, 17, 18, 19, 21, 22, 23, 26
Lincoln, Nancy Hanks, grave, 20
Lincoln, Robert, 20, 21
Lincoln, Sarah Bush Johnston, 19
Lincoln, Sarah Bush Johnston, grave, 20
Lincoln, Thomas, 16, 17, 18, 19, 20, 22
Lincoln, Thomas, grave, 20
Little River, 84
Little River Lumber Company, 68, 72, 74, 76, 77, 88, 89, 103
Little River Railroad, 68, 73, 75, 77
Little River Railroad Museum, 77
Little Tennessee River, 144, 145, 148, 153, 154, 157, 170
Llewellyn, M. V., 33
logging, 46, 65, 66, 67, 68, 72, 73, 74, 76, 77, 81, 89, 100, 103, 114, 124, 144, 156
logging camps, 75, 76, 83, 87
Lost Colony, The, 172
Louisiana Purchase of 1803, 12

M

Mack, Laura, 94
Maples, Thomas Filmore, 33, 35, 37
Maryville College, 125
Maryville, Tennessee, 2, 4, 6, 121, 145, 153
Masa, George, 100, 132, 133, 134, 135, 136, 137, 138, 139, 141, 142, 143
Masa, George, death, 138
Masa Knob, 139, 143
Mason Lumber Company, 76
Massey Business College, 125
McCoy, George, 141
Methodist Church, 57, 119, 122, 129
mining, 46, 100, 103, 144
Mitchum, Robert, 59
Montreat Junior College, 126
moonshine, 51, 52, 53, 54, 57, 58, 59, 60, 62, 63, 64, 88, 104, 149
Moore County, Tennessee, 63
Mountain View Hotel, 111, 112
Mount Cammerer, 166
Mount Guyot, 166
Mount Kephart, 104, 143
Mount LeConte, 105, 107, 165
Mullendore, Dialtha Melinda, 25
Mullendore, Laura Enloe, 25
Mullendore, Robert Bruce, 24
Mullendore, Roger Lafayette, 24
murder, 29, 35, 40, 47
Murfree, Mary Noailles, 55
Museum of the Cherokee Indian, 179

N

NASCAR, 59, 60

Nashville, Tennessee, 8, 35
national park proponents, 100, 101, 103, 114, 115, 128, 137, 138
National Park Service, 79, 83, 86, 116, 129, 143, 163, 165
national park vs. national forest, 103
Native Americans, 4, 8, 10, 12, 13, 79, 136
Nelson, Thomas A. R., Jr., 36
Newfound Gap, 115, 139, 161
Newman, Sam, 88
News and Courier, 56
Norwood Lumber Company, 76
no true bill verdict, 29, 34

O

Oakley, Wiley, 105, 107, 108, 109, 110, 111, 112, 113, 114, 115, 116
Oakley, Wiley, death, 116
Oak Ridge, 153
Oconaluftee Village, 178
Oconoluftee, 15, 16
Oconoluftee Visitor Center, 16, 79
Ogle, Lucinda, 117
Ogle, Noah "Bud", 109
Ogle, Rebecca Ann, 109, 110
Ogle, William "Black Bill", 87
Old Abrams, 119
Oliver, John, 119
Oliver, John Walter, 57, 125, 126, 128, 129
Oolooteka, 3, 4, 7, 8, 9, 10
organized crime syndicates, 58
Osage, 10
Our Southern Highlanders, 91, 97, 137

Outing, 96
Ozmer, Roy, 139

P

Pack Memorial Library, 142
Pearl Harbor, 144, 158
Pigeon Forge, Tennessee, 24, 25, 28, 165, 167
Plessy v. Ferguson, 31
"Poor Child," 50
Populist Movement, 31
Porter's Creek Trail, 139
Primitive Baptist Church, 57, 119, 121, 122, 124, 125, 129
Principal People, 79
Proctor, Tennessee, 76, 81, 82, 83
Prohibition, 58, 62
Putnam, Elizabeth Hannah, 44, 45, 46, 47, 48, 49
Putnam, Jane, 44
Putnam, Joe, 44
Putnam, Roberta Ann, 40, 45, 46, 47, 48
Putnam, Will, 45, 47, 48, 49
Pyle, Ernie, 115

Q

Qualla Arts and Crafts Mutual, 175
Qualla Boundary, 108

R

railroads, 31, 38, 68, 70, 73, 81, 83, 89, 110
Ramsey, Julia, 28
Reagan, Richard, 87
Redmond, Lewis, 52, 54, 55, 56

Remington Arms Company, 102

Republic of Texas, 1

Ritter Lumber Company, 67, 74, 76,
81, 83

road to nowhere, 156, 158, 160, 163,
164, 167, 168

*Roamin' and Restin' with the Roamin'
Man of the Smoky Mountains*, 116

"Roamin' Man", 105

Roanoke Colony, 172

Rockefeller, John D., 115, 138

Rogers, John, 4

Rogers, Tiana, 4, 7, 9, 10, 11

Rogers, Will, 108

Romines, Huse, 29

Roosevelt, Franklin, 115, 116,
158, 165

Roosevelt, Theodore, 92

Rose, Aquila "Quil", 62

S

Sasser, Jim, 163

"Save Our Smokies", 161

Scripps, J. S., 17

Seely, Fred, 134

segregation, 31, 151

Sequoyah, 170, 181

Sevier County, Tennessee, 27, 28, 29,
31, 32, 35, 38

Shay, Ephraim, 71

Shenandoah National Park, 138,
165, 172

Shuler, Heath, 164

Silent Spring, 162

singlings, 61

skidders, 71

Skyline Drive, 165

Sky-u-ka Hotel, 88

Skyway, the, 160, 161

Smith, Kate, 115

Sneed, Llewellyn, 28

Sneed, William, 29

Southern Railroad, 68

Spanish-American War, 38

splash dams, 70

Sports Afield, 96

Springs, John, 29, 36

Stanbery, William, 11

Stanley, Maurice, 50

stereotype, mountain people, 55,
97, 113

stills, 52, 57, 58, 61, 63, 64, 108

St. Louis Mercantile Library, 94

Stone Mountain, 166

Storie, J. C., 76

Sugarlands, 87, 88

Sugarlands Visitor Center, 87,
89, 165

Sutton, Marvin "Popcorn", 60

Swain County, North Carolina, 121,
158, 164, 168

swampers, 73

T

Tallulah Mound, 181

Taylor and Crate Lumber
Company, 67

Tennessee Valley Authority (TVA),
146, 147, 150, 154

Thomas, Will, 171

Thompson, Nancy Enloe, 16, 24

Thoreau, Henry David, 96

Thunder Road, 59
timber cruiser, 66
Tipton, Catlett, 35, 36, 37, 38
tourism, 25, 60, 64, 88, 89, 101, 102,
    111, 113, 127, 133, 134, 159, 160,
    165, 172
Townsend, Tennessee, 36, 68, 73, 77,
    89, 124, 160, 163, 166, 167
Townsend, W. B., 68, 84
Trail of Tears, 7, 108, 171, 179
Tremont Environmental Center, 75
Trentham, Levi, 86
true bill verdict, 18
T'Sali, 171
Tuckaseegee River, 80

U
Unto These Hills, 173, 174, 175, 178

V
Vanderbilt family, 134
vigilantism, 27, 32

W
Wade, Bob, 35
Walland, Tennessee, 68, 89
War of 1812, 1, 5
War of Texas Independence, 1, 12
Warriors of AniKituhwa, 180
Waynesville, North Carolina, 41
Wears Valley, Tennessee, 36, 167
Wells, Philip, 23

Western North Carolina Associated
    Communities (WNCAC),
    172, 176
Whaley, Laura, 34, 35
Whaley, Molly, 35
Whaley, William, 34, 35
whiskey runners, 60
whitecapping, 28, 32, 33
White Caps, 28, 29, 31, 32, 33, 34,
    37, 38
White Oak Flats, 88, 107
White Oak Flats Cemetery, 116
White, William A., 8
Whitting Lumber Company, 76
Wigwam Neosho, The, 10, 11
Wild East, The, 101
Wilderness Act of 1964, 162,
    163, 168
Williamson, Eli, 28, 29
Will Rogers of the South, The, 115
Wilson, Charlie, 73
Wolfe, Tom, 59
Wonderland Club, 84
Wonderland Park Hotel, 84, 86
woodhicks, 74
World War I, 58, 127, 145
World War II, 81, 89, 144, 158, 161,
    165, 171
Wright, Frank Lloyd, 124
Wynn, E. M., 29, 33
Wynn, Pleasant "Pleas", 35, 36, 37, 38
Wynn, William, 37

ABOUT THE AUTHOR

Michael R. Bradley taught US history at Motlow College in Lynchburg, Tennessee, from 1970 to 2006. He has hiked and camped in the Great Smoky Mountains National Park for sixty years, and is now taking his grandson into the park for his first hikes. Bradley is the author of three other Globe Pequot titles: *It Happened in the Great Smokies*, *It Happened in the Revolutionary War*, and *It Happened in the Civil War*.